BUILDING THE JAPANESE HOUSE TODAY

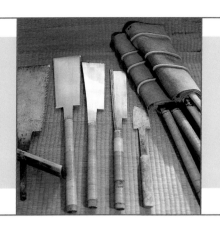

BUILDING THE JAPANESE HOUSE TODAY

by Peggy Landers Rao
and Len Brackett

Photographs by Aya Brackett

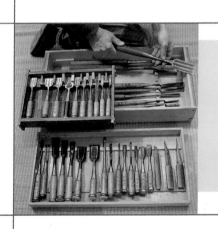

Harry N. Abrams, Inc.,

Publishers

Project Manager: Elaine Stainton
Editor: Jeffrey Hunter
Designer: David Noble
Production Manager: Norman Watkins
Jacket Design: Mark LaRiviere and E.Y. Lee

The authors would like to thank Ray Furse for his generous help in bringing this
book to publication.

All photographs by Aya Brackett, with the exception of those appearing on the
following pages: Len Brackett: 178; Nicholas King: 163; Kurt Lorenz: 19 (insert);
Brian Pawlowski: 10; Jeffrey Westman: 28, 59, 72.
All drawings by Timon Phillips of East Wind, Inc., with the exception of the
drawing by Aya Brackett on p. 77.

Library of Congress Cataloging-in-Publication Data

Rao, Peggy Landers.
Building the Japanese house today / by Peggy Landers Rao and Len Brackett;
photographs by Aya Brackett.
    p. cm.
 Includes appendices, glossary, and index.
 ISBN 0–8109–5931–3 (hardcover : alk. paper)
 1. Architecture, Domestic—United States—Japanese influences. 2. Architecture,
Japanese—United States. 3. Architecture—United States—21st century.
4. House construction—United States. I. Brackett, Len. II. Brackett, Aya. III. Title.

NA7208.2.R36 2005
728'.37'0952 dc22

                    2005004597

Printed and bound in China
10 9 8 7 6 5 4 3 2 1

Harry N. Abrams, Inc.
100 Fifth Avenue
New York, N.Y. 10011
www.abramsbooks.com

Abrams is a subsidiary of   LA MARTINIÈRE
                                         GROUPE

CONTENTS

Introduction

When Len Brackett returned to the United States twenty-five years ago after an apprenticeship as a temple carpenter in Kyoto, he built a traditional Japanese house for his family. Friends commented that it was so beautiful it belonged in a museum. Initially he was pleased to hear the compliment; later, he realized it wasn't good news for a builder who hoped to make a living building Japanese houses in America. Although visitors admired the house, it wasn't what contemporary Americans wanted. For the first time since starting his apprenticeship, he understood that his clients didn't want to live in a cold, dark, damp, and drafty house of sixteenth-century Japan, since these houses had no central heating, insulation, weather stripping, thermal glazing, or even convenient cooking facilities—all expectations of American homeowners. Brackett decided that unless he could discover how to make adaptations to the woodworking tradition he had been studying, he wasn't likely to find clients for the houses he'd been trained to build.

Yet he also firmly believed it was a tradition well worth continuing. For hundreds of years, generations of master carpenters have been repeating its honest lines and building intimate structures bonded to the outdoors. Frank Lloyd Wright, Walter Gropius, Charles and Henry Greene, Gustav Stickley, and other architects in the Arts and Crafts movement, all took inspiration from the elegance of Japanese design. Japanese architecture appeals as much to the mind as to the eye. An architecture of restraint, it blurs the distinction between inside and outside space, offering views of the changing seasons from many vantage points. The outer landscapes seen from within are arranged as microcosms of the natural world. This

Hidden in a backyard in California, a small guesthouse/art gallery exemplifies the finest in Japanese craftsmanship and the latest technical developments in modern comfort. (Photo by Brian Pawlowski.)

Introduction

When Len Brackett returned to the United States twenty-five years ago after an apprenticeship as a temple carpenter in Kyoto, he built a traditional Japanese house for his family. Friends commented that it was so beautiful it belonged in a museum. Initially he was pleased to hear the compliment; later, he realized it wasn't good news for a builder who hoped to make a living building Japanese houses in America. Although visitors admired the house, it wasn't what contemporary Americans wanted. For the first time since starting his apprenticeship, he understood that his clients didn't want to live in a cold, dark, damp, and drafty house of sixteenth-century Japan, since these houses had no central heating, insulation, weather stripping, thermal glazing, or even convenient cooking facilities—all expectations of American homeowners. Brackett decided that unless he could discover how to make adaptations to the woodworking tradition he had been studying, he wasn't likely to find clients for the houses he'd been trained to build.

Yet he also firmly believed it was a tradition well worth continuing. For hundreds of years, generations of master carpenters have been repeating its honest lines and building intimate structures bonded to the outdoors. Frank Lloyd Wright, Walter Gropius, Charles and Henry Greene, Gustav Stickley, and other architects in the Arts and Crafts movement, all took inspiration from the elegance of Japanese design. Japanese architecture appeals as much to the mind as to the eye. An architecture of restraint, it blurs the distinction between inside and outside space, offering views of the changing seasons from many vantage points. The outer landscapes seen from within are arranged as microcosms of the natural world. This concept is so integral to the Japanese understanding of shelter that the ideogram for "home" is composed of two characters: *ka* for "house" and *tei* for "garden." Only the inclusion of a garden makes a house a home.

Uncluttered interiors and minimal furnishings convey a sense of calm, a retreat from the world's demands. The visitor is never overwhelmed by a display of costly furniture or yards of expensive fabric. The construction itself is admired, along with the varied textures of materials, diffused light, and playful shadows. Left exposed, the building's bones become its decoration and its hallmark. Western woodworkers in particular marvel at the sophistication, precision, and strength of the joinery of these timber frames held together without metal fastenings. The various joints, perfected over centuries, regularly withstand the destructive forces of typhoons and earthquakes.

Each construction detail of a Japanese house is an expression of the concept of *osamari*, a word that conveys the idea of "unity," "integrity," or "effortless fit." Much of the frame of the house itself becomes the finish, along with such features as ceilings, cabinetry, doors and windows, shoji, and transoms. The sizes and proportions of these elements fall within a complex and considered system of dimensions and relationships to each other to assure a natural and easy flow of detail to all pieces. Nothing looks rough or unfinished, even in a barn.

The West, of course, had its own long tradition of timber framing, but the technique began to decline in the nineteenth century with the development of the waterwheel and the steam engine, which made the power to operate a saw cheap and available and gave birth to the sawmill. Milling dimensional lumber became easier than hand-hewing logs for a timber frame. The new sawmills made it easier to construct houses without the skills and knowledge of timber framing, and architectural forms in America began to change. Standardized 2 x 4 or 2 x 6 studs could be quickly nailed together for the frame. Later the use of gypsum board for the interior walls and plywood for the exterior also made the construction of a strong structure relatively easy.

Stud structures, however, generally aren't as long lasting as timber frames since nails rust and the structural connections loosen; ridges supported by stressed trusses sag; stud-framed walls go out of plumb. One might think such eventual weaknesses would lead people to build timber frames instead, but this is not the case. In recent decades a house has become a commodity, something to be bought and sold. It's no longer seen as an investment for succeeding generations of a family because so few original owners remain in their homes for a lifetime, and even fewer expect their heirs to live there. Unfortunately, when stud construction became common in the West and the skills of the timber framer were no longer in demand, timber framers stopped teaching, and their techniques often died with them. Until about twenty years ago, timber framing as a construction process in the United States was essentially dead. Then builders like Ted Benson, Ed Levin, and Jack Sobon among others resurrected timber framing, reinvented it, and launched a new industry. While timber framing doesn't seriously challenge the market supremacy of the stud-framed building, it has now become a viable alternative in America.

According to an architectural study sponsored by the Swiss-Asian Foundation, only 29% of the housing units in Japan in 1998 were timber frame, compared to 86% in 1963. This is due in part to the government's legislation requiring strict fire-protection modification of wooden buildings. The survey further reports that 78% of the Japanese polled reported they would prefer to live in traditional timber-frame houses. Yet, throughout Japan beautiful old houses are repeatedly torn down and replaced with ugly concrete or mortar-plastered structures. All this occurred because of the commonly held Japanese perception that the older house can't be adapted to be comfortable, convenient, secure, or fire-resistant.

In 1980, Brackett began a second apprenticeship in Japanese architecture, this time without any teachers except his American clients, who demanded the comforts and conveniences of the conventional home. What he has learned is the subject of this book. This examination of his construction of a guesthouse in California and the presentation of photos of other Japanese-style houses in the United States demonstrate that the superb craftsmanship begun in Japan, handed down through the centuries and respected by woodworkers the world over, can continue to grow and assume new forms here in America.

Hidden in a backyard in California, a small guesthouse/art gallery exemplifies the finest in Japanese craftsmanship and the latest technical developments in modern comfort. (Photo by Brian Pawlowski.)

DESIGN

I

A DECEPTIVELY SIMPLE COTTAGE is tucked into the backyard of a home in California. Sheltered by towering trees, it is notable for two reasons. Although built in the twenty-first century, it exemplifies classic Japanese architectural techniques and proportions refined over hundreds of years. Yet it also incorporates contemporary technologies and technical innovations for maximum comfort and energy efficiency. On entering the cottage, one's first sensation is the delicate fragrance of the cedar. Since the wood is unsealed, its fresh scent will last for decades. The finely planed surfaces invite touching, much like fine furniture. Visitors run their hands over the various woods—Port Orford cedar, sugar pine, Western red cedar, English walnut, and American chestnut—and exclaim at their glass-like smoothness. The building is a small, private joy, giving no hint of its existence to passersby on the street. Why and how was it built?

This book explains its construction—or more precisely, its evolution. The aim of this book is to demonstrate that Japan's extraordinary architectural tradition can be a realistic choice in the modern world by presenting that process in detail, supplemented with examples from other Japanese-style houses built in the United States.

THE OWNERS

It all began when Brian Pawlowski and Aki Ueno bought a three-bedroom house on a third of an acre in a pleasant neighborhood of medium-size homes. The couple liked its style, derived from French and English cottages, but regretted that it lacked a guest room. Rather than add on to the main house, they decided to build a guest cottage with a Japanese feel where they could display their Japanese woodblock prints. The oddly shaped lot, only 50 feet wide but 308 feet deep, made expansion in the form of a detached cottage a practical solution. An architect was lined up and paid a retainer.

Then one day Brian was out shopping, and the plans changed overnight. While Brian's purchases were being rung up, the shop owner took a phone call. Browsing idly while he waited, Brian came across a book about various Japanese homes that had been built in the United States. It fell open to the work of an American builder named Len Brackett, whose fine craftsmanship was shown in several photographs. Brian added the book to his purchases, read it through that night, and the next morning e-mailed Brackett at the address he found in the book's appendix.

Brackett turned out to be a rarity in woodworking circles: an American who had trained for five years in Japan with temple carpenters, whose sophisticated techniques are admired worldwide. When he returned to the United States almost thirty years ago, Brackett established a company specializing in traditional Japanese architecture, design, and woodworking—East Wind (Higashi Kaze), Inc., headquartered on a plot of private land in a national forest located in the foothills of the Sierra Nevada Mountains in eastern California.

Both builder and client became interested in Japan while still in school. Brian was drawn to Japan during his high school years in New Jersey, where he started reading about Eastern philosophy and Zen Buddhism in particular. He began a study of the Japanese language in college and since then, while pursuing a technology career, has continued to explore the culture's many diverse avenues, including its remarkable architectural joinery. In 1984 he read an art book on Japanese woodblock prints and was immediately drawn into their subtle world.

THE BUILDER

Brackett, a Minnesota native, studied at Reed College in Portland, Oregon, a school known for producing original thinkers. He felt at home on Reed's woodsy campus, where he majored in literature and Japanese studies. He, too, had an early interest in Zen Buddhism. For two summers during college he practiced Zen and was the zendo cook at the renowned Tassajara Zen Mountain Center, located inland from Big Sur on the Central California

Coast. The daily practice of Zen Buddhism had been part of his routine for years and resulted in a deep interest in Japan. After graduating from Reed, he decided to head west to the Far East and then continue around the world—never anticipating that his first stop, Japan, would be his only one. Before he set out, he collected enough money from friends to establish a bank account with a healthy balance—a requirement for a visa to Japan. The year was 1970, and this stipulation (which has since changed) was designed to discourage visiting hippies. As soon as he had received his visa, Brackett—who certainly looked like a hippie at the time, and shared many of the views of the hippie movement—returned the money to his friends and arrived in Osaka with three hundred dollars in his pocket, an open mind, and no real idea of what he wanted to do in life. Nor was he very concerned about it.

In dark December with landscaping dormant, the little cottage reveals its classic proportions.

The guesthouse entryway connects the two wings and offers an immediate view of the outdoors. Integration of the outdoors is a key feature in Japanese architecture.

Both wings of the guesthouse have a view of this small garden tucked between them. Seclusion in a small pavilion as a stage for experiencing nature is a recurring theme in haiku.

From Osaka Brackett went on to Kyoto, where he found a part-time job teaching English. After a time he began to practice meditation at one of the sub-temples of Daitokuji—a thirteenth-century temple complex that is a jewel of Zen architecture and houses many national treasures. This particular sub-temple emphasized "lay practice," daily *zazen* for those still living in the outside world, and seemed the perfect opportunity for Brackett, since it was close to where he was staying and he simply wanted a place where he could do morning and evening meditation with others, without becoming a monk.

Daitokuji is a temple of the Rinzai sect, strongly associated with the arts and the samurai class of old Japan. Within its boundaries are twenty-six sub-temples, each in its own walled and gated compound with gardens as impressive as the architecture The discipline in the training center, the *sodo*, is bone crunching—long hours of *zazen* and little food.

As time passed, Brackett became friends with many of the monks. Occasionally, some of them would climb over the temple walls at night and show up at his place, which they knew to be an always-open refuge, calling out at any hour "*Sake aru ka?*" "*Furo aru ka?*" ("Got any sake, got a bath?") Even though he had work the next morning, Len would dutifully get up, welcome them, and prepare the bath, since in winter they were usually half-frozen. Then he would feed them, because they never seemed to have enough food, and, of course, have a drink with them, although in those days he didn't like drinking.

In allowing the outsider to join in the meditation, Kobori Roshi (*roshi* is an honorary title for a Zen master) explained that since the *zendo* (meditation hall) wasn't large, he expected Brackett to use it. Otherwise, he was preventing someone else from doing so. Having been accepted, Brackett was expected to come every day and be on time. Commitments are not casual in Japan.

Len spent part of each day in this extraordinary setting. "It took my breath away, it was so astonishing. Until that time I had never been interested in architectural space, because I had never been anywhere that affected me like that. It was almost as if one could see the air enclosed by the building, could almost touch it—something like the way one can see the air outside on a damp, cool morning. The cathedral at Chartres has the same effect on me. Space becomes something positive; it isn't just empty, it's really *there*. Wouldn't it be amazing, I thought, to be able to build such sublime spaces? Now, thirty years later, I realize that there are very few architectural spaces like these."

Brackett's reappearance day after day apparently impressed the Zen master, who eventually inquired why he had come to Japan and what he wanted to do there. Brackett hadn't any particular plan, but was beginning to think that a study of temple carpentry might be interesting. Without hesitation, he heard himself saying, "I want to study temple carpentry." The Roshi's response was even more surprising: "I can introduce you to the best carpenter in Japan." That sentence led to an apprenticeship that changed the course of Brackett's life.

In time, Brackett learned that Kobori Roshi, who spoke almost perfect English, had gone to Stanford University before World War II. He had seen Daitokuji rebuilt and maintained with the help of wealthy Americans who were distressed that it had fallen into disrepair long before the war. Brackett believes that Kobori Roshi felt a certain debt to Americans and wanted to help those who he believed were responsible and serious about studying Japanese culture.

After Brackett had been allowed to sit at the temple he discovered that those who practiced there were welcome to come during the day to work, taking care of the gardens, making repairs, cleaning, and so forth. He had plenty of free time, so he often went to the temple. Frequently he was invited to dinner in Kobori Roshi's private family quarters. Despite his eminent position in the Japanese Zen world, Kobori Roshi lived a simple and disciplined life, and dinner was usually cooked over an open fire pit in a room next to the kitchen. Before eating, the young visitor would be invited to sit around the fire, drinking sake with the Zen Master, his disciples, and family. In addition to being a Zen Master, Kobori Roshi was also an urbane and sophisticated man, a calligrapher, the grand master of the Enshu School of Tea, a landscape painter, a scholar of classical Chinese poetry, and a craftsman in his own right—a potter. The Zen master knew almost everyone who was anyone in Japan, including the emperor and the prime minister. It was at his temple that Queen Elizabeth and Prince Philip stayed when they visited Kyoto in the 1970s in a guesthouse built especially for them. The American college boy had fallen in with some heady company.

There by the open oak fire, Kobori Roshi would take Brackett's hand. Holding it in his two, he would gently growl that it was a craftsman's hand, big and strong, "Fine hands for a carpenter! How skilled these hands might some day become!" Kobori Roshi had a high regard for craftsmen and artists and was respected in the world of Japanese craftsmen. He was a friend of Shoji Hamada, Kawai Kanjiro, Bernard Leach, and the Raku family, the family that developed and still produces raku-ware pottery.

Brian, of course, didn't know anything about Len's background when he contacted East Wind. (Brackett's rigorous and lengthy carpentry apprenticeship in Kyoto is described in chapter 7.) The prospective client simply described his location, his site, and his goal—constructing a detached structure that would serve as a quiet retreat. Brackett asked the Pawlowskis how large a building they envisioned and how much of it they wanted to be traditional Japanese architecture. They replied that they wanted a small building with the timber frame construction and intricate joinery of Japanese architectural design, but with hardwood floors instead of tatami (straw mats), so that they could use a limited amount of furniture They also wanted it to include a small office, and, most important—for Aki, who was born and raised in Japan—it had to have a traditional Japanese bath.

Brackett then invited the couple up to the East Wind shop in the Sierras so they could meet the staff and get a fuller understanding of this kind of architecture. Approximately half the construction of a traditional structure is done in the shop, where all the wood components of the timber frame are prepared and the joints cut for assembly later at the site.

When the visitors saw the meticulous work and beautiful wood involved, they could readily picture a Japanese structure in their backyard. They were also impressed to see a sample of Brackett's earliest work, his own two-thousand-square-foot house that stands nearby. A visit to the workshop either helps galvanize clients' commitment to a project or allows them to decide early on that a Japanese home isn't for them. East Wind maintains an extensive library on Japanese architecture, and all the drawings and critical path schedules from past projects are on hand for viewing. Brackett says, "This kind of work is really different from most building projects. Unless potential clients have had experience in Japan they probably would never really 'get it' without seeing it."

After the workshop visit, the Pawlowskis dropped their original architect and were eager to embark on the design process with East Wind.

The Site

The next step was a joint visit to the proposed site. In the backyard where the new structure would be placed, several mature redwoods and six Monterey pines presided over shallow soil holding fruit trees dying in too much shade. Brian wanted to keep the larger trees and transform the area into a Japanese garden when the building was finished. Both the narrow site and the requirements of the town's planning and building boards

were on Brackett's mind: "What kind of building would be permitted here? A guesthouse, or should it be called an office, a meditation space, a utility structure?"

The site added to the design challenge since it was in a town where the building and planning codes were particularly stringent. Height limitations were especially irksome. No part of the building was allowed to pass through an imaginary line made at the property boundary starting six feet above grade and slanting up at a 45-degree angle into the lot. This rule ensured that a new house would not block neighbors' sunlight. The structure also had to be set back from the property line six feet on both sides, reducing the 50-foot width to only 38 usable feet. Since the cottage was located in a 100-year flood plain, the minimum elevation of the floors had to be 31 feet above sea level. These requirements placed restrictions on height and size, and ultimately led to building the house on a slab, something Brackett wasn't keen on because Japanese buildings are usually slightly elevated, but there was no escaping the codes. Brian was grateful that Doug Tweed, East Wind's general manager, saved money by getting competitive bids.

East Wind also found to their consternation that "heritage trees"—that

Brackett built his first house in the United States for his own family in 1980 with a single helper, his friend and first apprentice, Walter Hardzog. The smaller photograph (by Kurt Lorenz) shows the bones of the house during construction.

is, redwoods and live oaks—anywhere near the foundations had to have their roots exposed using an "air spade," (compressed air) to ensure they wouldn't be damaged when digging foundation trenches. "Of course, everyone wanted to protect the trees," Brackett said. "No one wanted to build a house with a view of these beautiful specimens and kill them in the process. But the last thing to do is dig up their roots, with or without an air spade, and expose delicate feeder roots to the drying sunlight. This was dutifully done at a cost of thousands of dollars, as the silviculturalist waved his hands like a necromancer and declared that the trees were okay." All the while Brackett sat on the sidelines muttering, "Yes, they may be, if you haven't killed the damned things digging them up!" Then every tree on the lot had to be surrounded with a chain-link fence for protection during the construction process.

Size and Cost

When builder and client addressed the topic of cost, it became clear that they could work together. "Without their understanding of the finances involved, it would be a pretty expensive hobby for me," Len explains. He is more passionate craftsman than businessman, and in his flannel shirt, patched jeans, and suspenders, he has the air of a pioneer from the early days of settling the West.

He explains that three factors are central to the cost of any house: client's budget, number of square feet, and cost per square foot. The essential formula is cost (budget) equals area (number of square feet) times cost per square foot (dependent on quality and degree of detail). A large budget allows for either a larger house or a more expensively constructed house. When the cost of building a design exceeds the client's budget, then either the size of the house or some of the expensive elements (or both) must be reduced to bring the entire structure back into budget range.

There are a number of variables to be considered within this decision-making process. Small buildings are more expensive per square foot than large ones for a number of reasons. A large percentage of the work in Japanese architecture is in the milling and layout of the pieces. Once the planning has been done and machinery for this work has been set up, the actual cutting proceeds with relative speed. Since three-quarters of the time in accomplishing any task is planning, organization, choosing and allocating lumber, and setup, and only a quarter of the time is spent in actual cutting, doing more of the same task means increased productivity and less cost per piece. Additionally many of the expensive elements of any building, such

A typical Japanese bedroom can be 9 x 9 feet and still feel spacious.

as site preparation, permits, travel expenses, and plumbing and electrical installation represent more-or-less fixed costs not strictly tied to the size of the building. An electrical panel, for instance, costs nearly the same for a house of four thousand square feet as it does for a house of eight hundred square feet. That means the cost of the electrical panel per square foot for the smaller building is several times higher than for a larger one.

Even though reducing overall square footage reduces space, Brackett invariably encourages clients to build a smaller house than they first envision, making it as beautiful as their budget allows. And he continually urged the Pawlowskis to do this. "I kept increasing size, he kept pushing back," Brian says. "Glad I won sometimes."

Though reducing the size reduces costs, small structures present a distinct design challenge. They are absorbed so fast visually, it is difficult to make them intriguing or surprising, a characteristic of many great buildings. Unexpected views, unusual doors to storage spaces (where children love to play), gardens inside a house, hidden rooms, all add character and interest to a design. The larger the building, the more complex the floor plan can be, providing an almost geometric increase in the number of opportunities to include interesting design elements.

One way to limit space (and cost) and yet preserve a feeling of spaciousness is to use tatami mats, without Western furniture, in the entire house or parts of it. If Brackett's clients had been interested in living in strict Japanese style throughout the cottage, space could have been used more efficiently and the overall square footage reduced. Furniture requires considerable space to function properly. A dining-room table, for example, also requires space for its chairs, room to move the chairs out, and sufficient open area to walk behind them. Many dining rooms also include a sideboard or a credenza, which also require the space they occupy and additional room to move around them comfortably and open their doors.

The Pawlowskis had vetoed tatami in favor of furniture because Brian was concerned about his mother's comfort when visiting. (Sitting on tatami flooring for long periods is uncomfortable for many who are accustomed to sitting on chairs and sofas.) Even though there would be hardwood flooring throughout, the Pawlowskis would still ask visitors to remove their shoes, to protect the floors and to keep the place clean. They also ban shoes in the main house—a result of Aki's upbringing in Japan—and they find that people are very accommodating. Shoes ruin both tatami and the softwood floors of traditional Japanese homes, which are finished only with a hand plane.

The Pawlowskis did save considerable square footage, however, by choosing a Japanese bedroom for the guesthouse. Let us consider, for example, the requirements for a Western bedroom with a queen-size bed, five feet wide by seven feet long. With two bedside tables eighteen inches square, furniture alone occupies a space eight feet wide by seven feet long. To make the bed, at least two additional feet on both sides are needed, for an area twelve feet wide; when an additional three feet are added at the foot of the bed, the room must be twelve feet wide by ten feet deep. Adding a dresser at the foot of the bed requires three more feet, making the room twelve feet wide by thirteen feet deep, or 156 square feet—the minimum space for a Western bedroom.

The Japanese bedroom, however, devoid of permanent furniture, can be considerably smaller. In the traditional Japanese house, futon, clothing, and other possessions are stored in a built-in closet about three feet deep that runs the length of the room, freeing the floor space for other activities. In this arrangement, an area nine feet by nine feet—eighty-one square feet—is perfectly adequate for sleeping, and in fact feels generous. But even a mere fifty-four square feet will serve in a pinch. What's more, any tatami

Opposite page: The sleeping area in the guesthouse can be closed off for privacy. A futon replaces the table on the tatami platform, which is 9 x 9 feet. The *toko-noma*, the traditional display alcove, is in the foreground.

room in the house, even a study or an office, can become a sleeping room simply by spreading a futon on the floor at night.

Eventually, the Pawlowskis added tatami to a large platform in the nine-by-twelve-foot sleeping room. This allowed them to make the room multiuse, accommodating a low table to entertain floor-seated guests on the tatami platform without covering the entire floor with tatami. They decided that a bed would have limited the room to the single function of a place to sleep, which represented only a fraction of the time spent in the cottage.

Shoes On or Shoes Off and Other Design Considerations

One of the distinct benefits of tatami rooms is that they liberate the owner from the need for most home furnishings. The visual and aesthetic focus is the architecture and its link to the garden, not the contents of the space—what we call interior design—such as furniture, fabrics, art objects, and their overall integration. The structural framework is left exposed, its bold lines uninterrupted by furniture. The graphic lines of the tatami's dark borders echo those of the vertical posts, the shoji grids, and ceiling structure, intensifying the room's geometric character. In fact, the entire house can be seen as layer upon layer of grid patterns. Then, amid all this geometry, exceptions appear. These may be a naturally round post, a board with a bark edge, a round window or even a window shaped like a gourd.

If shoes are to be worn indoors, the floor must be tough, and that means a choice of masonry, tile, stone, hardwood flooring, or other traditional Western floor coverings such as carpet or linoleum. Since such floors don't invite sitting, furniture is needed, and furniture dictates a dramatic change in the approach to design. It is possible to place furniture on tatami, setting pads under their legs to protect the mats, but Brackett says it doesn't work well and it feels strange.

Combining furniture and tatami creates another problem: if some people are sitting on tatami and others on furniture, their eye levels are different. In ordinary situations, we are more comfortable if those we are sharing space or conversing with are on about the same level. Even more important, the eye level is critical to making a building *feel* right, since windows or glass panels in sliding doors have to be placed so that occupants can see the ground outside from a seated position, whether on the tatami floor or on furniture. Furniture elevates eye levels 16 to 18 inches—the height of a chair seat—and windows are aligned to correspond.

The *engawa*, the narrow veranda or corridor of the Japanese house, was a place to sit and enjoy the garden. Opening its doors brought the outside in.

One way to incorporate a tatami area in a Western house with furniture is to elevate the tatami area so that the eye level is consistent with the furniture height. Brackett has devised a similar solution for adding an *engawa*—the wraparound veranda or corridor so characteristic of Japanese architecture, where people sit on the floor—to a room with furniture (see chapter 6). Since the *engawa* is a central element in the transition between the garden and the interior, Brackett is committed to keeping it in Westernized houses and making it work: "There has to be an *engawa* or the feeling of the Japanese house is gone."

In hybrid Japanese-Western houses, where shoes are worn in part of the house, this transition still occurs at the threshold between hard flooring and tatami or softwood floors. Such subtle changes of elevation are found in Japanese architecture, whether homes or temples, as one steps up through several levels of admission and transition from outside to inside space. From the garden path there is a short step up into the entryway (*genkan*), an intermediary space that is semipublic, since vendors and other strangers often have access to it. If the guest is invited into the house, he removes his shoes, places them carefully out of the way and, using the step-up board, moves up

An entryway in a Colorado Zen monastery has a slate floor and a cherry step-up board. Its sliding glass door is faced with a wooden grid to make it more formal and to provide some privacy.

Another typical entryway viewed from the interior. A shaped, natural stone serves as a bench to remove shoes. Built-in cabinet for coats and shoes has woven walnut doors.

another 18 inches or so to the wooden floor area, where he will be provided with house slippers. After a few more steps, he meets another slight vertical rise to the tatami area, where he sheds the slippers to walk in stocking- or bare feet on the straw mats. A visit to the toilet involves once again donning house slippers when stepping out into the softwood corridor, leaving them outside the toilet door, and stepping into a pair of toilet slippers for use in that room only (and heaven help the person who forgets to switch back from the toilet slippers to house slippers!). Should he want to view the garden via the *engawa*, he goes through another transition, stepping down onto a stone step after slipping on exterior sandals.

Brackett emphasizes these soft transitions between interior and exterior in the houses he designs, whether Westernized or traditionally Japanese, making them central to the entire design.

Entirely or Partially Japanese

Another way to reduce building costs is to construct only high-priority rooms—a central core or a wing—in the Japanese style, while employing a more conventional design and standard materials in constructing the util-

Wisteria vine ties a bamboo window. Traditionally, a grid like this of heavier split bamboo was used for the lathwork under the plaster.

Window of cattails, tied with wisteria. Surrounding plaster was made with soil taken from the site.

The circular window, flattened like the setting sun, provides a welcome relief from the rectangular lines of this house in northern California. The bench under the window is also a desk. Sitting on the floor is no problem because the middle doors open to a heated well for the legs.

One East Wind client commissioned a Japanese-style barn, which is used for pressing olive oil and making wine. During other seasons, it's an artist's studio. The floor is stained concrete.

Although the barn's doors look delicate, they are 5 ft. wide, 11 ft. tall, and strong enough to endure 100-mph gale winds that whip around the site.

ity and lower-priority areas. After all, one doesn't need a Japanese broom closet, utility room, storage room, or laundry room. Prospective home builders are advised to order their priorities, deciding in which parts of the house they spend most of their time. Some people live in their kitchens; others may spend hours in a combination bedroom-office; or they may be drawn to the veranda in the summer. A partially Japanese house is a very workable solution if the budget is limited.

For example, one couple realized that they spent a lot of time in the master bedroom, their refuge in a house full of teenagers. They wanted a separate wing for the master bedroom suite with a Japanese bath and a large walk-in closet. East Wind did the design work for the wing and consulted with a local architect, who designed the rest of the house so the two parts fit together. East Wind built the master bedroom wing, while a local contractor built the rest of the house according to the architect's design.

Another client asked East Wind to concentrate the Japanese construction in the entryway, the living room, and a tower providing a view of the surroundings. These rooms became the central core of the house. The company designed a simplified Japanese timber frame in a cheaper lumber for

Opposite page: In Brackett's own home, the built-in desk under the window provides a view of the garden. See Appendix page 194 for the desk's construction details. (Photo by Jeffrey Westman.)

the basic wall structure, which was erected by Pacific Timber Frames of San Luis Obispo, and then supplied a third contractor with finished and ready-to-install materials for ceilings, bay windows, some of the doors, and some of the barge rafters, to give the roof its characteristic Japanese shape.

Building a partially Japanese house is a strategy that has been widely adopted in contemporary Japan, particularly in two-family homes, where parents live with their eldest son and his family. In such cases, it is the senior members of the family who occupy the Japanese-style rooms. Many modern single-family homes also routinely incorporate one Japanese room with tatami because of the strong attachment Japanese have to their traditional domestic architecture.

The Pawlowski's detached guesthouse allowed its owners to isolate their Japanese preferences in a structure all its own, creating a special-use space that didn't have to accommodate other living needs. Over the years East Wind has built a variety of separate structures—places to meditate or do yoga on tatami, or work at home surrounded by nature.

ROUGH FLOOR PLANS

Modules

In discussing the plan for the guesthouse, Brackett explained that all traditional Japanese structures are based on a design module that derives from the size of the tatami mat, essentially six feet by three feet. This module, called a *ken*, is the key to maintaining the characteristic proportions of Japanese houses, and it was the design basis of the guesthouse even though tatami were not going to be used. East Wind is unusual in that it invites prospective homeowners to do their own initial layouts based on this module. This way the client can take the lead instead of merely accepting the designer's ideas. Brackett believes that the role of the designer and craftsman is to work from the clients' wishes and suggest improvements that they may not have considered.

Client's Priorities

Brian and Aki made their drawings on graph paper, using a scale of a half inch to three feet. With the three-foot module plan, room dimensions would be in increments of 3 feet—for example, 6 x 9, 9 x 12, 12 x 15 feet, and so forth—positioned in an arrangement that best suited their needs. They had been asked to make quick, unmeasured sketches of any features they might want, from lofts to swimming pools. They were to give every idea a

hearing, no matter how unreasonable it might seem. They were cautioned not to put effort into finishing any of the designs until they had made many sketches. Brackett says, "There is a natural tendency to become attached to a plan that you have worked out in great detail. This can hinder the fluidity of the design process, and it is easy to become 'trapped' into a design that doesn't suit your purposes or that, in fact, you don't even like very much."

The couple began by indicating the position of the major trees and the desired location of the guesthouse. In drawing the structure, their thinking evolved. They abandoned the idea of including an office and replaced it with an art workshop and gallery. Eventually, it became clear that three main rooms and the bath would accomplish their goal.

When they had made about ten sketches, Brackett asked which they liked best and what elements they liked in the others. This not only provided a specific design to start with, it also gave the builder an insight into their thinking. Patterns in their designs became apparent, such as round

Room size is indicated by number of tatami mats, the traditional floor covering, whose dimensions, combined with the width of one post, are the ancient design module for Japanese houses. This home is in the foothills of the Sierra Nevada Mountains.

windows and the layout of the Japanese bath with the adjacent dressing room. For Brackett, how the client wishes to live in a house is more important than their initial specific requests. He has noticed that many clients express one kind of expectation, but their designs reveal something else. For example, they may *say* they want a big house with a big view, but then they design a series of houses that ignore the big view and put a distinct emphasis on a tiny contemplative garden in back.

One element Brackett is partial to is an entryway that leads immediately outside again. He suggested an entry with double, full-length, glass "back doors" that offered a view and access to a back garden. Eventually it was decided that such an entry would be the core of the guesthouse and would be flanked by two wings. The final size of the building was set at 888 square feet, just under the limit of 900 square feet established by local regulations for detached accessory buildings. The east wing became about twice as long as the west because it contained the art gallery plus the Japanese bath, a changing room for the bath, the toilet, and the utility area. The west wing was designated "meditation space," with a sleeping room, a sitting room, and a raised *engawa* seat to look across to the rest of the house. Brackett tends to favor a building that provides a view looking back on itself, which can be more interesting than those with only a view out. An attractive opposite wing not only contributes to a richer view, it also creates a space for a tight little garden that in effect becomes a part of the house.

The couple wanted the cottage to be wholly Japanese yet efficiently modern. Their priorities included high, vaulted ceilings with the roof's support structure revealed, controlled natural light for the gallery with harmful ultraviolet rays screened out, and storage space for the art not on display. "It was expensive," Brian remembers, "but it was all my choice. At every point Len explained that features such as an open ceiling and a complex roof added to the price. Len and Doug did a great job of trying to drive costs down. They were very frugal."

One of the artists represented in the homeowner's growing ukiyo-e collection is Masami Teraoka, a contemporary artist who now lives in Hawaii. Some of Teraoka's works are eight to ten feet high, so the gallery needed eight-foot walls to satisfy the collector's hope of one day owning a large-scale piece: "Teraoka encapsulates my relationship with Japanese culture and architecture. His principal body of work is the use of ukiyo-e imagery and iconography to explore the relationship between East and West. Introducing Western themes into this art is an anachronism, just like the cottage. This cottage belongs to the past, but is thoroughly contemporary in comfort."

Instead of graph paper, some East Wind clients use dominoes as a design tool, since like tatami they have a length to width ratio of two to one, and they can be easily manipulated to experiment with layouts. Some of the tiles, though, have to be sawn in half to make half-tatami-mat modules that also occur in these houses.

A couple in Marin County took the dominoes suggestion one step further. They used colored tiles to indicate relative square foot costs: red for the least expensive rate, black for more expensive, and gold for the costliest. The general contractor's areas of the house were red; East Wind's were black; kitchens and baths, usually expensive, were in black or gold, depending upon the plan chosen; and the traditional Japanese bath was in gold. Tinkering with the design became fun, like playing a board game. Using dominoes, of course, requires making a paper record of the design. The tiles also tend to slide around, but they are helpful in deciding what should be put on paper.

On occasion, a client's unlikely or even outlandish design can be realized. The tower mentioned above came about that way, even though such an element usually isn't found in traditional Japanese homes. It has a 360-degree view of the whole Sacramento Valley to the south, Mount Shasta and Mount Lassen to the east and north, and the Siskiyou range to the west.

Meeting Homeowner Expectations

Brackett maintains that his clients are his best teachers. He thinks the Pawlowski guesthouse bath is his best ever. Its design originally came from the client, who made an outlandish demand—that the corner post, where the tub was to be positioned, not extend down to ground level, because he wanted an uninterrupted view of the garden from the tub's corner windows. Brackett thought the request was outrageous and explained that since it was a timber-frame building each post was essential. "How do you expect me to build a house with a corner post missing? What's going to hold it up?" He was told, "That's your problem. You're supposed to be the designer and builder, so figure it out."

The solution was a short corner post supported by a system of cantilevered beams above the ceiling. This hanging post stops just below the top edge of the two corner window openings. A window head without tracks and a flat sill were installed between the two posts flanking the opening. The actual tracks and windows were mounted on the exterior, beyond the plane of the posts and walls, an unusual arrangement. The open windows could be slid on the outside wall almost past the opening.

One client protested that the crucial corner post and windows in the bath interrupted the view of the garden. He insisted that they be eliminated. The solution has become an East Wind hallmark and is a feature of the guesthouse. The windows are mounted on the exterior, outside the plane of the posts and wall.

With neither post nor window interfering with the view, it is easy for the bather to feel the tub is in the garden. The windows interlock at the corner, and locking one window locks them all.

Brackett never saw this corner arrangement in Japan, although he freely admits that others may also have thought of this. It's a design he has used since in other buildings, including the Crestone Mountain Zen Center in Colorado. He confesses that some of his best designs have come out of what he considered unreasonable demands.

The very idea of a designer dictating to the client is anathema to Brackett, and he has a thorough disregard for the "artist" who refuses to do what he's asked for reasons of personal pride or insistence on being "creative." Brackett strongly believes in the Japanese tradition that the craftsman should remain nameless and never impose his taste on a client or be led by his ambition for professional recognition.

He analyzes his role as follows: "The national treasures of the world were usually designed by craftsmen, not artists or architects. Even the great artists of the Renaissance were considered craftsmen, hired to complete the design of a palazzo wall, decorate a church ceiling, or create stained glass windows. The Gothic cathedrals and the Greek temples of Europe were designed and built by masons; the National Treasures of Japan were designed and built by carpenters. Of course, the craftsman's self-expression is an essential component, and inevitably his way of doing his work will distinguish his work from others and even make it identifiable, but this usually isn't intentional. What makes it possible at all is the support of the patron or, in the case of homes, the clients who pay for them, who will have to live in them, and who have the right to make demands. The carpenter is the one with the skills and the tools to figure it out. He should have a deep knowledge of what he does, the aesthetics of it, its history, and understand not only how something is made, but also *why.*"

Kobori Roshi once commented to Brackett that he was lucky to be a carpenter, since he could always do things for others, and not all livelihoods allowed that. For instance, he said, "If you're a Zen priest, unless you are an *exceptional* Zen priest you aren't probably doing anybody any good, and you end up simply being a parasite. A great Zen priest can really help others, but not all priests can be great. As a carpenter, however, you can always contribute something, even if you aren't particularly skilled. You can at the very least make a chicken coop . . . something that people need."

Brackett says: "East Wind is interested in building houses *for people,* not for the bank, not for local realtors, and not to make the neighbors feel bad about their own houses or what they represent." The features of a Japanese house are supposed to unfold gradually, just like a Japanese garden, where the winding paths conceal the full view, letting the visitor discover its charms one by one. Only one East Wind house has ever been resold, and in that case the new owner asked Brackett to remodel it for his specific needs.

An ingenious simplified plan of a house, drawn with bamboo pen and ink on a board. Even today many skilled Japanese carpenters use boards like this as their only building guide, and some still do. East Wind used this one in 1985 for a house in Marin County, California, in addition to conventional plans.

2 PRECISE DRAWINGS

ONCE A PLAN FOR THE GUESTHOUSE was agreed upon, it was still too early to start the precision drafting process either by hand or computer. Brackett simply looked at the couple's plan and let it ferment in his mind. He has always found that a considerable waiting period produces better plans than those arrived at in a rush. This gestation period allows the homeowners to work out their needs and desires and to use him to help them design their house as they bounce ideas off one another. The process usually takes at least two months, and it isn't uncommon for it to last as long as nine. It took about three months for the guesthouse. Generally speaking the larger a house, the longer it can take. One client was in this process for almost a year, although that's longer than usual.

As the basic design was refined, ideas went back and forth. "Uh-oh, this door swings the wrong way." "I don't like the way the access to the bath works; can't we move the door to this side?" There was a problem with the entry. A normal entry has a vertical step up of about 12 to 18 inches, "But we've got this thing built on a slab with everything almost on ground level. That will never do," Brackett said thinking out loud, "because there isn't any step-up demarcation point to take off shoes. What should we do, lower the slab in the entry or raise the floor? Well, flood control won't allow the slab to be less than so many inches above the flood plain, and if we raise the house, then we exceed height limitations, so how about lowering the entry slab and making it look as if it is *outside the house* by not putting the doors on until after the house is signed off." This, of course, was said in fun, but Brackett is always aware of advice he got from the very first building inspector he worked with, who said that sometimes calling an element that is not allowed something else gets it approved. Brian appreciated that "Len and Doug certainly knew how to address Western building codes without compromising the integrity of the traditional Japanese timber-frame construction. That experience is what makes them so valuable."

Finally the floor plan sketches were refined enough to start precise drawings, which could be expected to reveal problems not apparent in the original plans. An initial design was done using AutoCAD (computer-aided design) to make a 3-D model. More refinement sessions ensued, this time with East Wind taking the lead in designing the roof and exterior elements of the building and getting client approvals as the plan became more and more detailed. The designs were originally sent as hard copy, but Brian eventually bought a copy of Volo View from Autodesk, makers of AutoCAD, which allowed them to save paper and production time and shortened the period for the couple to review changes during the initial flurry of designs. Brackett determined such things as roof pitches, sizes of all components of the house, layout of ceilings, kinds of doors, and other details. Since this part of the process requires a thorough understanding of Japanese architecture, homeowners usually don't get involved with it; they are unfamiliar with the components required and haven't any idea about their size or shape. The Pawlowskis, like most East Wind clients, were content to let East Wind determine what was needed.

The process closely approximates what carpenters in Japan have been doing for hundreds of years. In the old days, the owner and the carpenter worked out a floor plan together, and then the owner retreated and let the carpenter take it from there. Most owners didn't presume to be able to dictate the finishing details or even discuss them with a skilled carpenter. However, today, there are people—engineers, building departments, other contractors—who have to know exactly what the house will look like and how it will be built, so exact floor plans are necessary.

As expected, the precise drawings yielded new problems. Two closets were planned for the meditation wing, but one had to be eliminated because a shear wall was needed where closet doors were indicated, and because the foundation required for the closet would have come too close to one of the redwood trees, possibly damaging its roots. Not enough space had been allotted for the water-heating equipment, since the city wouldn't allow any

part of it underground. To solve the problem, the ceiling in the utility room was eliminated so that some of the mechanical hardware could be installed in the roof structure, and permission was obtained from the city to use an underground waterproof chamber to house the pump.

In choosing a heating system, forced air was rejected because it is too noisy, creates hot, dry spots that damage artwork on paper, and is inefficient with such high, vaulted ceilings. Hydronic or radiant heating, which employs warm water in plastic tubes under all the flooring, was chosen. It had the beneficial side effect of making it comfortable to walk

Two round windows, slightly flattened, dominate each wing of the guesthouse. By night they cast their own moonlight.

A built-in chest at the end of the gallery stores art and conceals several appliances for entertaining. Turn to page 172 to see the doors open and the appliances.

about the house without shoes, and was also a better choice for the preservation of the woodwork and the few pieces of fine furniture that would be used. The temperate California coastal climate precluded the need for air-conditioning.

Hydronic heating is becoming increasingly popular since it is even, silent, energy efficient, and requires little maintenance. This, however, was a new frontier for Brackett. How would a heated sub-floor affect the wooden floor? Surely serious shrinking would result if the floorboards were nailed down. The conventional practice is to install a floating floor attached only to itself, which can expand and shrink without creating gaps between the planks. Since East Wind had never done a floating floor, a specialist would be subcontracted.

WINDOWS AND VIEWS

Traditional windows generally aren't very big—frequently only a couple of feet high, and very rarely three feet or more—but Brian wanted the round windows on the front of the cottage to be large. About six feet in diameter, they were designed when the room was going to be an office, their lower edge dropping below a stand-up desk. When the space became a gallery, their height was still right for guests moving about looking at the art as well as for providing a view of the garden.

The windows presented an early design disagreement. Brackett thought two identical windows would be too much, and he recommended that one be an interesting shape latticed with reed, but Brian planned on using landscaping to break their strict symmetry, so Len relented. One wing was set back to make the façade more interesting and the distorted "H" plan created space for the courtyard garden. When someone approaches at night and the house is illuminated inside, the large windows provide an inviting glimpse of the joinery in the roof and some of the other architectural elements.

The windows in the sleeping area were positioned so that a person resting on the low platform made for the futon can view the garden. Eight five-foot-high sliding glass doors were designed to sit flush with the top of the platform at one end of the room, four on each side. In the sitting room, two windows were placed just high enough to fit a couch underneath them.

In the design process, the couple considered many ways to bring cross ventilation into the gallery without forfeiting valuable wall space. They finally decided to put windows very high on one side, well above the normal height for displaying art.

In the Japanese snow country, the *yukimi* shoji slides up so those sitting on the floor can see the snow settling on the surroundings. In East Wind's version, an insect screen can be interchanged with the glass window to adapt it to the California climate. The photo on page 25 shows the same shoji with the panels closed.

In some cases, windows are placed to *restrict* the view to a small garden, blocking a look beyond, and sometimes they are positioned to guard privacy. Too big a view can be overwhelming and detracts from the feeling of peace, safety, or privacy. For example, a Westernized Japanese house in Tiburon, California, has a sweeping view of San Francisco Bay. Brackett built the house on spec to launch his company and lived in it for a while before selling it, but he found the constant panorama was too intrusive. Sometimes he wished for less drama, less distraction. One approach for achieving this is to frame the view so that it changes constantly depending upon where one sits. He remembers Eiheiji, an ancient Soto Zen temple in Japan situated in an old-growth cedar forest surrounded by amazing views. One of the most impressive sights is a mountain peak visible only through a small window at the end of a long corridor. The building could have been designed to face this impressive peak, but it wasn't. Rather, the builders chose to frame the view, much like a painting; this way it doesn't intrude, and the result is stunning.

Partial or framed views are often considered more intriguing and charming, so Brackett advises that designer and owner together calculate the line of sight from a seated posture to make sure the eye falls naturally on the desired focal point, preferably on a long view if there is one *and* on a small garden for more contemplative moments. The window can be raised for the big view and dropped for the smaller one.

GARDENS

The small garden between the bath and the meditation wing was planned to be the focus of the guesthouse, central to the entry, and visible from the bath, the sitting room, and the sleeping room. Although this garden would have paths running through it, the typical Japanese residential garden is too small to be a strolling garden. Its main function is to present a serene picture to be enjoyed on a daily basis from the comfort of the interior.

The usual practice in the West is to regard the home and garden as separate entities, with the garden designed after the house is built. In Japan, however, the garden is an integral part of the design, no matter how small the plot. This attitude of merging inside and outside space can even be seen in the word for "home" in Japanese. It is composed of two characters: *ka* for "house" and *tei* for "garden," demonstrating that that without a garden, a house is not a home. Brackett's own home encircles a garden, which is its central focus.

Tatami's Long History

Archaeologists have found that as early as 300 B.C. thin rice-straw mats were used in Japan for various utilitarian purposes, fashioned into numerous items such as baskets, carrying bags, ceremonial flags, fishing nets, and even burial cloths. In the third and fourth centuries A.D., when development of wet-field cultivation turned rice into a major commodity, tatami became commonly used as sleeping mats. The length of the tatami mat, roughly six feet, was determined to comfortably accommodate a sleeping adult, and its width was dictated by the average length of the strong root end of the reeds from which they were made. In the fifth century the widespread use of iron tools made the production of mats easier.

As thicker mats were made, the tatami began to be used as a floor covering. Documents that describe the enormous Buddhist temples built in the fourth and fifth centuries mention their great halls as having been covered with eight hundred or even one thousand tatami. Japan's oldest extant history, the eighth-century Kojiki, reports the existence of tatami craftsmen, who by then were making four different qualities of mats. During the Heian period (794–1185), imperial and high-ranking households began to use their sleeping tatami as sitting mats as well, since the tatami was portable in those days. Gradually the mats multiplied on the floors of their homes. The teahouse made its appearance in the Muromachi era (1333–1568), and tatami were used to cover its entire small floor area, spreading the tatami's popularity to the samurai and merchant classes. By the sixteenth and seventeenth centuries the mats were in wide use in the homes of commoners, gradually "carpeting" whole floors in the main living areas. The versatile uses of the tatami may help explain why Japan is the only major civilization to develop without a tradition of significant furniture.

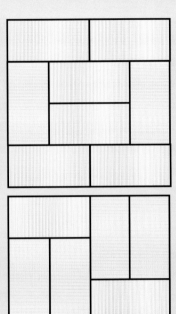

Tatami generally are about 2 1/8 inches thick, consisting of a dense inner core of tightly matted and bound rice straw (toko) covered with a goza, a finely woven mat of a kind of reed called igusa. The goza is generally bound with silk edging (heri). Borders are often black, but they can be blue, brown, or brocade. No longer portable, tatami now weigh about eighty pounds.

Tatami come in many qualities. Their cost is mostly related to the quality of the goza, which comes in ten or more grades. (The straw core comes in a few grades as well.) Hand-woven goza, so tightly woven that water barely penetrates them, are the most durable. The finest mats are made only from the root ends of the reeds. Cheaper mats use the entire reed, are machine woven, and don't last nearly as long.

The tatami has become a ready measure of space. Rooms are described as a six-mat room, an eight-mat room, or a ten-mat room and so on, with the number of mats also dictating the height of the ceiling. Tatami size varies slightly by region, but their width is always exactly half their length. The standard Kyoto tatami is 3.15 feet by 6.3 feet. In Tokyo, they are smaller, closer to 3 feet by 6 feet. With the advent of high-rise, steel-reinforced concrete buildings, the mats have been reduced in size. The 8-inch-thick wall of the new buildings is much thicker than the traditional post of the Japanese house. Instead of expanding the dimensions of the floor of apartment rooms to accommodate standard tatami, builders placed the thicker walls on the standard centerline spacings of the traditional house, thereby reducing the interior dimensions of the room. Because tatami can differ in size, different six-mat rooms can vary considerably in actual area. For the purposes of this book, we will use the Kyoto tatami (kyoma), one of the largest in Japan and the one generally used by East Wind, since it seems more fitting to the American scale.

STORAGE

Storage is always a prime issue in any house, and it must be considered from the outset. One of the two closets in the entryway was designed to hold coats, shoes, and other things. Another storage area was built into the end of the gallery. It was designed to resemble an oversize Japanese chest, a *tansu*, to store art.

To be genuinely hospitable, a guesthouse needs a place to make coffee or tea or to serve cold drinks. Rather than tuck a kitchenette into a closet or an alcove, a portion of the *tansu* was dedicated to concealing an espresso machine, a sleek bar sink, a microwave, and a small Sub-Zero combination refrigerator, freezer, and ice maker, creating an entertainment center that reflects the Japanese ingenuity for using every inch of space to the maximum.

THE BATH

The traditional Japanese wooden bathtub was to be custom-made by Robert's Hot Tubs in Richmond, California. Though the clients decided they wanted a tub four feet by three feet, Brackett is always trying to convince clients to build smaller tubs. This is partly because the idea of the "California hot tub" has never been attractive to him. Not only does it take long to heat up, he finds the sanitizing chemicals in most of them unpleasant, "like bathing in a bottle of bleach," he says. He feels hot tubs use far too much energy and an unnecessary amount of water. Our California couple, however, wasn't going to be persuaded to scale back; they would have the tub they dreamed of. (Brian is larger than the average Japanese.)

DECORATION AND DETAIL

Brackett warns against adding excessive detail throughout a house, even if the client can afford it. Sometimes a home with fewer extra decorative elements such as elaborately carved *ranma* (wooden transoms), gable detailing, woven ceilings, and so forth can be more pleasing aesthetically. Restraint is the essence of this architecture; detail demands attention, and too much can be overwhelming and undermine the feeling of serenity. He says, "These spaces are supposed to give the inhabitant energy, not take it away. At the most extreme, imagine living in the Louvre or in the Metropolitan Museum of Art. Most people can't handle so much beauty too long." Years ago Brackett went to a client's house that was filled with

Rembrandts, Picassos, and Brancusi sculptures everywhere. "After about two hours I just wanted to find a couch and lie down and go to sleep. I was exhausted just being there!"

To Brackett a simple mud-plastered wall is every bit as beautiful as a fresco, just as a room with a single painting in the *tokonoma* (small display alcove) can be more satisfying than a room resplendent with art. One or two perfectly formed objects in a space creates an elegant and restful mood, while a room filled with knickknacks, even beautiful knickknacks, can be unsettling.

THE KEN MODULE

The six-foot module used for the guesthouse plan—the *ken*—is the basic unit of an ancient and ingenious system of building design. Japanese structures have never been designed by architects, who only made their appearance in Japan at the end of the nineteenth century, when Western building materials and techniques were first introduced. The pleasing proportions of the Japanese house evolved from a pragmatic approach to building, developed by carpenters starting in the seventh century.

By the end of the fourteenth century in Japan, the principal support posts in residential architecture were positioned between 6 feet to 7.5 feet apart. At that time, the span between post centers was the design module for the rest of the building, a concept derived from the ancient rules of proportion employed in Buddhist temple architecture in China. Once it became customary to use tatami as a floor covering, the tatami were placed so that they stretched between the surfaces of the posts (not to their centers). In the late seventeenth century, the tatami's length was standardized at approximately 6 feet, and carpenters began to use its fixed length along with the standard post dimension to position the posts on a grid. The tatami in combination with the posts became the design module known as the *ken*. One *ken* now equals the length of the tatami plus the width of half a standard post at either end. The span between the posts is expressed in terms of *ken*—1 *ken*, 1 $^1/_2$ *ken*, 2 *ken*, and so forth.

Therefore, the size of the tatami in a local area *and* the size of the post in the particular home determine the precise size of the *ken* in that building. The locality in Japan usually dictates a particular tatami size, so within that locality it isn't flexible. But the post size is, for it is dependent on the size of the house, its location in the house (*engawa* posts are smaller than standard posts, for example) and the style of architecture—residential, teahouse, or farmhouse. Sometimes one wing of the house will be executed in a different style architecture and have posts that differ in size from the posts of the rest of the house. In such a case, one of the main building posts is designated as the "standard post" for the house as a whole, and it will determine the *ken* for the entire house no matter what size post is laid out with it.

The size of the post has a dramatic effect on the total volume of lumber needed for construction, since the dimension of all other components of the house is tied to the post dimension (see chart on page 49). Increasing a post from five to six inches actually necessitates nearly fifty percent more lumber. As a result, if lumber is expensive—as it is in Japanese architecture—the post size becomes an important financial consideration

The standard post for the Pawlowski guesthouse was fixed at 0.37 *shaku* (a unit of Japanese measurement), or about 4 $^7/_{16}$ inches square and the tatami length chosen was 6 *shaku* (about 71 $^9/_{16}$ inches), the length of the Tokyo tatami. This is slightly larger than would be used in Japan for a structure of this size, but it allowed for a thicker wall to hold insulation, wiring, and other utilities. Therefore the *ken* for the guesthouse was 6 feet 3.996 inches.

Rooms with tatami almost always have dimensions that are multiples of half a tatami, a three-foot square. Consequently, logs to be milled or used in their natural form can be cut in advance in the woods to appropriate *ken* and half-*ken* lengths with a minimum of waste. Even scrap generated in the building process is usable, as it will always be in units of *ken*. With the design module measured from post center to post center, tatami are automatically accommodated and always fit faultlessly. Since tatami extend to the side of the post facing the room and not beyond it, there will also be space between the posts for sliding door tracks separating adjacent rooms.

While the *ken* system determines the floor plan, the ceiling height is determined by the number of tatami in the room (the total area) and the type of architecture—home, temple, or teahouse. (Area does not determine the height of a room with an open roof structure like the guesthouse, which has no ceiling, only the finished underside of the roof.) As rooms increase in size, the height of the wall surface between the door heads and the ceiling (the *kokabe*) becomes greater, so the ceiling height is determined by adding together the height of door head, the *kokabe*, and the height of ceiling molding.

In order to keep the doors as low as possible for proportional reasons and yet prevent a taller-than-average Westerner from hitting his head, the

Formula for kokabe, *the distance from door heads to dropped ceiling*

Number of mats	Room dimensions	Traditional kokabe height
4.5	9 x 9'	1.2–1.5'
6	9 x 12'	1.8–2.0'
8	12 x 12'	2.4–2.5'
10	12 x 15'	3.0'
12	12 x 18'	3.5–3.6'
15	15 x 18'	4.0'

doors in the guesthouse were set at 6.5 *shaku,* about 6 feet 6 inches, off the floor. In a stud-frame Western house the average door is 6 feet 8 inches. Brackett likes to keep the door heads as low as possible, remembering that the traditional Japanese house has heads that are only about 5 feet 8 inches. Since this is clearly too low for the West, Brackett usually makes them 6.4 to 6.5 feet and never below 6.2 feet. Sometimes one exit door is made 6 feet 8 inches to satisfy building code requirements.

The chart above assumes the average East Wind door head of 6.5 feet, the door head (0.14 inches to 0.16 inches), and ceiling molding of about 2.25 inches to 2.5 inches.

The widths of the guesthouse doors and windows were also dictated by the distances between posts, since the posts serve as doorjambs in addition to supporting the roof.

From the fourteenth century, India and China were also employing complex systems of standardization in residential architecture, yet only Japan's module—with its intimate relation to human proportions, its uniformity, and its prevalence in all types of Japanese architecture—has endured. A number of Shinto shrines are dedicated to Shotoku Taishi, the imperial prince who is reputed to have brought to Japan the first craftsmen skilled in the Chinese techniques of carpentry, which the Japanese then spent the next fifteen hundred years refining even further. These shrines are considered by carpenters to be *their* shrines.

Heino Engel, in his classic work *Measure and Construction of the Japanese House,* calls the Japanese module "an extraordinary phenomenon in architecture without equivalent elsewhere."[1] He describes it as "a standard distance for construction and economy, a module for aesthetic order . . . a length related to human proportions. The *ken* is mainly the carpenter's

[1] Heino Engel, *Measure and Construction of the Japanese House* (Tokyo: Tuttle Publishing, 1985), p. 24.

achievement. No other feature in the Japanese house is likely to better demonstrate his mastership of the total range of his profession."[2]

Brackett takes issue with architectural writers who say aesthetics dictated these building practices. He believes that the module was created because it was practical; it made building easier. He asserts, "The inherent—perhaps fortuitous, even serendipitous—beauty of this *practical* system of building led to what we see, which is very beautiful, and happens to be one of the finest architectural aesthetics in existence. Japanese design results from how structures are built, that is, form follows construction method. The building's framework isn't concealed; it's the main event. If one is familiar with traditional Japanese woodworking technique and views that process as leading to works of grace, simplicity, and beauty, then one would naturally end up building either Japanese buildings or Scandinavian furniture. Both are simply expressions of the most rational way to put wood together so that the resulting structure is strong and efficiently executed."

KIWARI—WOOD ALLOTMENT

While the *ken* module established the floor plan for the guesthouse, another set of calculations known as *kiwari* determined the size of all its components. *Kiwari* (literally, wood allottment) is a guide rather than a firm law and is based on the dimension of the principal posts.

Kiwari dictates directly or indirectly the size of every other structural wood member. Their relationship to the post is shown in the chart on the facing page and extends to sills, heads, beams, king and queen posts (king posts support the ridge; queen posts usually support purlins and are generally shorter), tracks, lintels, hanging posts, tie beams, rafters, hip rafters, purlins, ridges, ceiling moldings, and stringers. While post size may differ within the house for special needs, as in a farmhouse where an enormous post can support almost the entire roof, the *ken* size remains constant throughout the building and uses the standard post. Clearly, the post is the most critical of all elements of the house. (The post, however, does not determine thickness of doors and windows; standard doors and shoji were used in the guesthouse.)

The sizes of some components *indirectly* derived from the post size are included in the chart on the facing page. These guides can be changed according to the aesthetic judgment of the individual carpenter, the materials available, load requirements, and the dictates of other structural

[2] Ibid.

Kiwari: *Dimensions of Structural Components in Relation to Post Size*

H refers to horizontal dimension of the installed component listed below. V refers to vertical dimension of the installed component listed below. % refers to percentage of standard post dimension.

The horizontal and vertical dimensiona are not to be confused with the standard procedure for indicating dimensions in lumber, smallest to largest, that is, thickness, width, length. The lumber can be installed in various orientations. A 2 x 4 member, for instance, can be installed on its edge, flat, or vertical.

Japanese name of part	English name of part	Thickness as % of post dimension	Width as % of post dimension
Honbashira	Main post, base post	100%	100%
Engawa hashira	Veranda post	80–90%	80–90%
Tatami shiki	Lower track for doors adjoining tatami	Thickness of tatami (vertical dimension), flush with top surface of tatami	100% H full width of posts, surface to surface. Shiki is coped to post 100%/H
Standard *kamoi*	Standard head	45-46%/V	100% minus post chamfer of both sides/H. Can be coped to post for formal work, then no deduction need be made.
Nageshi	Trim above heads—runs all around the room	Projects into room $\frac{1}{7}$ of post dimension	80-90%/V
Ranma kamoi	Transom head	30%/V	Well inside post chamfer/H
Ranma shiki	Transom lower track	30%/V	Well inside post chamfer/H
Mawaribuchi*	Standard ceiling* perimeter molding	Projects beyond post surface into room 4-6 bu ($\frac{1}{2}$ to $\frac{3}{4}$ inch)/H	45-50%/V
Sao*	Standard ceiling stringer*	40%-66% of height of *mawaribuchi*/H	100% to 140% of *sao*'s width
Keta**	Perimeter beams (heads)**	100% plus chamfer, 2-4 bu depending upon bottom chamfer size/H	200% or so, depending upon load of roof, style of architecture, etc./V
Moya and *mune*	Purlins and ridges**	75-100%/H	100-140% of width/V
Tsuka**	Queen posts**	60-80%	60-80%
Tsuri tsuka	Posts hanging from perimeter beams to support heads having spans exceeding 6 *shaku*	Inside chamfer of width of *kamoi* or less/ through the wall	About 80%/face
Kento tsuka	Support posts for window track or exterior floor beam coming up from below	Inside chamfer of width of *chujiki* or window *shiki* though the wall	About 80%/face
Hondaruki**	Main roof rafters**	40%/H	50% or so
Dodai	Sill	70-80%	100% or 100% plus chamfer, or inside chamfer of post (100% minus post chamfer), depending upon whether it runs into post or post rests on top of this member/V
Engawa taruki**	Veranda (lean-to) rafters**	80% (or so) dimension of main rafters	80% of the dimension of the main rafters
Tsunagi	Tie beams between main posts	50-60%/H	100 or 100 + %/V
Sumigi and *tanigi*	Hips and valleys**	Twice the rafter/H	Twice the rafters/V

* These thicknesses and widths are variable, depending upon the style of architecture, degree of elegance, location, etc. There are many versions of these components but the proportions remain basically the same.

** These items are structural and are also highly variable, not only for aesthetic reasons but because they must be sized to carry differing structural loads, such as snow, slate or tile roofing, or large tributary loads.

requirements. It also varies by locale or the lineage of the carpenter. Brackett elaborates, "Every carpenter takes his initial understanding from his teacher and from what he has seen, but we all do what we think looks best, with the result that to a discerning eye an individual's work becomes recognizable as distinctly his. Because I was a temple carpenter's apprentice, many of the details found in ceremonial architecture occur in my houses. Had I been a teahouse carpenter, I suppose more of the elements of classical *sukiya* (teahouse) architecture would be present."

Up to the late sixteenth and early seventeenth centuries, building techniques and the proportions of the *kiwari* system were recorded on scrolls kept by master carpenters and handed down through generations as family trade secrets. When a century of civil war ended in about 1600 and a more stable government emerged, building activity greatly accelerated. In order to keep up with the demand for new construction and train apprentices, master carpenters put the information in manuals, which were known as *hidensho* (secret hereditary writings). Brackett says, "We aren't so proprietary about such things today. I believe in disseminating knowledge, which is part of the reason for this book."

Every part in the guesthouse is close to the proportions recommended in the chart on page 49.

THE TRADITIONAL CONSTRUCTION BOARD PLAN

Before the advent of sophisticated design tools, Japanese carpenters managed splendidly through the centuries with an ingenious plan board called an *ita-zu* or *kanban ita*, a simplified plan of the house, drawn with bamboo pen and ink on a board about 12 inches high and 18 inches long. Most skilled Japanese carpenters used it as their only building guide, and some still do. Although draft plans are required today for both clients and building permits, East Wind sometimes finds the traditional plan board also extremely helpful. The board shows the centerlines of the posts and the walls, with the entryway side marked along the bottom.

Any point in the house can be indicated by the right-angle intersection of two centerlines. All the vertical lines are given letter designations. All horizontal lines are numbered. Any intersection then can be defined simply by using the intersection code—for example A4 or G7. (Intermediate locations can be described by using decimals for the numbered axis—14.5, for example, for a point midway between 14 and 15—and letters with a

Every component is coded in the shop with a number and a letter indicating its position and orientation in the building.

slash—such as B/C for a point between B and C.) These coordinates are marked on each piece of wood as it is precut in the shop.

The coding not only indicates the location of the component in the house, but the way it's written on the wood orients it for those assembling the house. Vertical members such as posts have the coordinates at the top of the surface that faces the entry side. If the coding is upside down when installed and viewed from the entry side, the piece has been installed upside down. If the writing faces the back of the house, then the post is rotated 180 degrees *wrong*. Coordinates of horizontal members are always written on their top surfaces—their upper sides—visible from a bird's-eye view above the entry. The coding will not show in the finished house because it is either written on the top of the tenon or on the bottom of a pocket cut in the post, both of which will be covered up in the building process.

For the traditional carpenter, the construction board plan functions as the plan for the house—though a very particular type of plan that requires much acquired knowledge and years of actual experience to read. It is akin to a musical score for those who have a long familiarity with music.

COMPUTER-AIDED DESIGN

In today's world, conventional floor plans must be done for those who have to know what's going to be built. The client, of course, wants to see the plans, and showing him a highly schematic construction board will clearly not do. Building departments also have to see plans before they will allow construction to go forward, and structural and energy engineers need a complete set of drawings to validate the building's structural integrity and energy efficiency.

East Wind began to use AutoCAD Architectural Desktop from Autodesk about five years ago to prepare the finished and very detailed drawings derived from hand-drawn sketches worked out by Brackett and the client in earlier design sessions. Initially, they made two-dimensional CAD drawings similar to hand-drawn plans, but later Brackett decided to take the plunge and invest considerable time and training to do the design work using CAD the way it was intended—that is, by making 3-D models, which allow the client to see what is almost a photograph of the design *before it is built.*

Brackett has some misgivings about CAD since drawing with computers is slow, taking about twice the time as drawing on paper. CAD may execute simple drawings faster than the conventional method, but the complex and highly detailed drawings that are uniquely possible with CAD require more time. Since the screen of a computer is small, constant zooming in and out is necessary to see details. But seeing precisely *where* those details are in the drawings is important, and this can be exasperating since it makes viewing the whole building time-consuming and annoying.

Nevertheless, there are other compelling reasons to use CAD. For one, it is much easier to make changes or to "flip" or rotate a building. CAD drawings can be readily transmitted via the Internet to clients, contractors, and inspectors. Another great advantage is that the 3-D models let the client see what's actually going to be built without mastering the art of envisaging a building from a blueprint. In addition, since CAD drawings are made laying down one layer over another, and since any given layer can be turned on or off, special drawings showing only certain sub-constructions are immediately available to show, for example, only roof components with rafters, purlins, short posts, and beam layers in place. This allows special drawings to be provided to those in the shop or to engineers, enabling them to understand the plans with greater clarity. In the long run, even though CAD plans take longer than hand-drawn plans, they save time and reduce the possibility of misunderstandings.

Timon Philips, a recent graduate of the Rhode Island School of Design, does most of the company's AutoCAD work, making superbly detailed three-dimensional drawings. Just as building a Japanese house turns out to be more than most aspiring carpenters expect, so too was using CAD to design it, but Philips found a way. Philips shares the CAD and drafting work with Doug Tweed, who did the 3-D CAD work for the guesthouse. "Doug keeps me out of trouble," says Brackett, "by handling financial issues too." Tweed brings to this artistic and commercial enterprise versatile experience, having been a successful contractor in his own right, the president of a tugboat company, and, for a while, after studying art in college, a professional potter.

The all-important floor plan (See Appendix page 193) determined all subsequent drawings. Then the following were prepared: elevations, important wall sections, a reflected ceiling plan, several layers of roof structure plans, foundation plans, site plans, roof sections, and detail sheets.

With the plans completed, an estimate of costs was drawn up and submitted to the Pawlowskis, who approved it with a few changes. A build contract between client and builder was then drawn up, and a building permit application was filed. The building department accepted the plans and the accompanying structural and energy engineering as complete, and a permit was issued with no objections—though the department did express a reservation about the plastering procedure, which East Wind adjusted to their satisfaction. (Plastering is discussed in Chapter 6 with plaster details shown on Appendix page 198.)

The next step was to choose the various kinds of wood for all the components.

Wood surfaces are finished only with the Japanese hand plane. They become smooth as glass, eliminating the need for paint, oil, sealer or wax. These shavings are from 0.002 to 0.005 inches thick.

3 · WOOD

IN TRADITIONAL JAPANESE architecture, the finished structure is rarely painted, stained, or oiled, although some elements of ceremonial and occasionally of residential architecture were lacquered. In contemporary Japan, lesser grades of wood are painted, but fine lumber is meticulously hand planed until it is as smooth as porcelain, its surface tight and impervious. Wood requires less preparation than stone, is cooler in summer, and is not as cold to the touch in winter, making it an appropriate choice for Japan's temperate climate. Instead of applying paint or other finishes, the country's builders relied on the absolute purity of the material for effect. Their goal was to reveal wood's finest natural qualities, which is why careful selection is crucial.

In Japanese construction, far more time is invested in choosing lumber than in cutting it into the various components. Wood is both the most prominent feature of the design and the central element in the décor of its residential architecture. The building process begins in the forest, where the carpenter carefully selects local trees, looking for the best logs to be milled into the finest lumber.

Strong, stable, and beautiful woods such as cypress (*hinoki*) and cedar (*sugi*) are preferred for traditional construction in Japan, but on the main island of Honshu—a real botanical treasure house—the builder has a huge variety of woods to choose from besides *hinoki* and *sugi*. Japan has one of the world's most genetically varied temperate forests. Cherry, zelkova, oak, chestnut, and a host of other genus and species are all available. In

Quality softwoods are used throughout and left exposed to be appreciated. In the Japanese house the focus is on the architecture, not the contents, possessions, or interior design. This house is in northern California.

southern Japan the builder can select from red cedars, several different species of pine (*matsu*), and many other woods similar to those found in the southern United States. In the north he uses hemlock, spruce, and fir, along with northern hardwoods such as oak, beech, and alder. Wherever he is, however, a Japanese builder usually uses what is locally available, and the wood for the guesthouse was selected the same way. However, today "locally available" can connote a huge area because of the relative ease of transporting logs and lumber.

The selection and preparation of lumber for construction reflect an important aspect of Japanese culture, where *discernment* is the key value in dealing with wood. The Japanese people have a remarkable ability to recognize and appreciate fine woods. Wood has always been the favored building material in Japan and every effort is made to use it to its best advantage. In his years in Japan, Brackett noted that even a deliveryman arriving at a customer's house might exclaim about a remarkable piece of wood that catches his eye. Although most of its old growth (trees over two hundred years old) is depleted, Japan still has one of the richest temperate forests in the world. Sadly, however, the country seems determined to ruin this great natural legacy through a combination of neglect and widespread monoculture tree farming of coniferous trees.

Brackett obtained most of the lumber for the guesthouse from two mills, one in Oregon and one in Canada. Oregon's outstanding Port Orford cedar was his first choice, as always, for posts, groundsills, eaves fascia detailing, doors, and windows. With its Japanese counterpart, *hinoki*, it is probably the finest softwood in the world. Working with Port Orford is a carpenter's joy. Its elegant, aristocratic grain and white luster enhance any structure. Port Orford heartwood was chosen for some of the windowsills and some of the purlins and ridges, as well as for the Japanese tub, where rot resistance and fragrance are important. Port Orford cedar would also be used for the shoji (sliding screens of wood and paper), as is usually the case in Brackett's homes.

Western red cedar supplied by the Canadian mill and incense cedar, available in the local Sierras forests, were earmarked for a variety of highly visible components, including all the suspended ceiling boards, finish roof boards, most of the door heads, all the wide board door panels, and a woven ceiling planned for the bath. Care was taken to find older pieces with fine grain.

Sugar pine from Oregon and from local independent loggers was lined up for the roof structure, including all the rafters, perimeter beams, most of the short posts, and the rest of the ridges and purlins. Brackett knew his friend Skyler Phelps, a specialty supplier in Auburn, California, would have English walnut for the important floor of the *tokonoma*, the alcove designed to hold a changing display of art, such as a scroll, a flower arrangement, or a treasured ceramic object. Phelps deals in figured walnut for gunstocks and sends various species of central California's highest quality logs to Germany, France, Italy, and Turkey to be sliced into acres of thin veneers. After some discussion, Brazilian cherry—not a true cherry, but a tropical hardwood—was chosen for the floors, even though Brackett would have preferred black cherry, a temperate wood. The Japanese aesthetic favors temperate softwoods and hardwoods, and tropical wood rarely has the handsome grain patterns produced by the seasonal growth of colder climates. Brackett also avoids tropical woods because he is reluctant to be involved in the terrible forestry practices common in the tropics.

WHITE CEDARS

Port Orford cedar (*Chamaecyparis lawsoniana*), found in the United States and Canada, is akin to *hinoki*, the Japanese cypress (*Chamaecyparis obtusa*). The American wood is indistinguishable from *hinoki* from the Bishu area of Japan, which is noted for its white wood. The heartwood of *hinoki* has a pinkish cast, however, while that of Port Orford cedar is usually creamy white. Their fragrance also differs, but with the possible exception of Alaska yellow cedar, all the woods of this family have a wonderfully clean, almost floral scent and are known for their rot resistance, strength, stability and beauty.

Port Orford, which is also called white cedar, Oregon cedar or Lawson's cypress, is native to the coasts of Northern California and Southern Oregon, and is the largest of the genus, which comprises six species worldwide. With *hinoki* in short supply in Japan, the United States has been exporting Port Orford cedar there for well over a century. Today's logs command very high prices. Most of the old-growth of this species remaining in the United States is on government land.

Hinoki, mentioned above, is a vital component of Buddhist temples and Shinto shrines; its white color appeals to the Shinto emphasis on purity. It is so respected that before trees are cut within the precincts of some important shrines, a priest clothed in ancient garb enters the forest and performs a lengthy traditional ceremony to enlist the help and approval of the gods. Very large old-growth *hinoki* specimens are extremely rare in Japan and a single log can be worth many thousands of dollars. Even younger logs are quite valuable. It is commonly grown in managed forests, where the limbs are regularly removed to produce knot-free lumber.

Taiwan hinoki (*Chamaecyparis taiwanenis* or *formosensis*), native to Taiwan and known as *taihi* in Japanese, grows to be very large and has extremely oily wood with a strong yellow cast. Old-growth specimens are also becoming increasingly rare in Asia; the enormous, ancient logs were commonly imported for Japan's best architectural work.

Alaska yellow cedar (*Chamaecyparis nootkatensis*) can be almost canary yellow and, like the others of the family, is particularly rot resistant, stable, and fine-grained. Some people think it has a musky, slightly unpleasant smell. This tree is found only in the higher elevations of northern California and in a band up through the Cascade Mountains all the way to Alaska. It, too, finds its way to Japan in large quantities.

Atlantic white cedar (*Chamaecyparis thoides*) is much smaller and knottier than other members of the genus, but like the others, highly prized for boat building.

When exposed to sunlight, Port Orford cedar, like its Japanese counterpart, *hinoki,* gradually darkens to a caramel color. In temples hundreds of years old, it can become almost black, resembling ebony. This unfinished *engawa* floor is twenty-five years old and is noticeably darker than the Port Orford used in the guesthouse. (Photo by Jeffrey Westman.)

The soaking tub and floor slats in this Bay Area house are Port Orford cedar, a kind of *hinoki*. Bucket is *sugi*, a Japanese cedar used for its fragrance, rot resistance, and stability.

Sawara (*Chamaecyparis pisifera*) is a Japanese wood similar to the white cedars but darker in color. It has a wonderful, spicy smell and is preferred for bathtubs in Japan. Like all members of this family, it is also very rot resistant, although it doesn't have the strength of many of its cousins.

Hiba (*Thuja dolobrata*), is found in more northerly areas of Japan and is also referred to in English as a cedar. It is very similar to the Alaska yellow cedar but sweet smelling, quite strong, and rot resistant. Though it looks and feels like a member of the *Chamaecyparis* tribe, it is more closely related to Western red cedar, from which "cedar" shingles are made.

These woods are usually used in Japan for ceiling boards, finish roof boards, door panels, mud sills, and the wooden components of the mud walls. With many of the same characteristics as the white cedars—rot resistance, spicy fragrance, flexibility, and beauty—they are also used for posts, rafters, and even door and window stiles and rails. These woods aren't particularly noted for their strength, but are much prized for their resistance to shrinking and warping.

Western red cedar and sugi. The traditional dark cedar used in Japan is known as *sugi* (*Cryptomeria japonica*), and has some similarities to Western red cedar (*Thuja plicata*), which is used for shingles, as well as to the incense cedar used in manufacturing pencils. Botanically, it is closer to redwood than to the dark American cedars, and like redwood, it is easily split. It has a characteristic peppery smell and is quite rot resistant. Since *sugi* isn't found in North America, East Wind uses Western red cedar instead. Both Western red cedar and incense cedar are very similar to *sugi*, and are used for all components normally made with *sugi* in Japan. Nicely "rubbery," Western red cedar can be bent more than most species without cracking. It is particularly desirable for ceilings, since it can be milled into thin, wide boards without much risk of warping or checking. Like *hinoki*, it can be used for shoji, but it is especially appropriate for intricate applications such as door panels as well as small objects like boxes and buckets. Because it is soft, warm, and gentle, unlike *hinoki*, which is bright, formal, and ceremonial, it has earned a dominant role in teahouses and teahouse-inspired architecture

Western red cedar is available from Northern California to British Columbia, but the Oregon variety tends to be faster growing and therefore doesn't produce as fine a grain. In addition, it is subject to attack by flat-headed borers, common in the southern region. It may look fine coming off the mill, but when planed, holes the size of a fountain pen can suddenly appear.

In Japan *sugi* comes in many grades ranging from inexpensive, low-quality wood used as concrete forms or packing material to a costly, high-quality grade for architectural use. It is, therefore, both the cheapest and most expensive lumber available in Japan—fineness of grain, color, and absence of knots distinguishing the most valuable from utility-grade lumber. When it comes from trees six hundred to two thousand years old, a single 12-foot ceiling board $3/8$ inches thick and 18 inches wide may cost a thousand dollars or more. One tree found on the island of Yakushima has a girth of 50 feet and has been estimated to be between three and seven

This log is called a *"shibori maruta,"* meaning "wrung out" like a towel. Natural ones like this are rare and treasured. Its remarkable skin was a surprise, discovered only when the bark was peeled.

A long vertical cut is made in some logs to relieve checking. The cut is usually positioned so it won't be seen. In the guesthouse, however, it has become a point of interest, inlaid with Port Orford cedar. Two-thirds of the way up, a knot that was halved in the cutting process has been recreated. Playful elements like this are common in Japanese architecture.

Opposite page: The natural round *tokonoma* post is carefully chosen for its beauty, historical significance, or its unconventional spirit, as in this house in the Sierras. The Douglas fir from which it was made was found growing at the site. The *tokonoma* flooring is myrtle, boardered by American chestnut. The curved member at the bottom of the wall is Pacific yew.

thousand years old. Yakushima is one of the very few places in Japan with a surviving natural old-growth forest. Though ancient trees survive in small groves or as individual specimens in the precincts of some shrines and temples, natural forests this age in Japan are gone. Like old-growth *hinoki* trees, ancient *sugi* trees are worth a fortune.

Sugi plays a very special role in the *tokonoma*. The front corner of this decorative alcove usually features a floor-to-ceiling, natural post that can be very expensive, often costing thousands of dollars. The finest posts come from trees in the Kitayama district of Kyoto, where they are carefully tended. Trees grow by adding layers to their exterior—a new ring every year and a spurt of vertical growth in the spring. When a limb falls or is removed, the point where it met the trunk remains, as a knot. As the tree adds new growth rings each year, they eventually cover the knot, hiding it inside the trunk, but even if it doesn't show on the log, it will become visible again when the log is milled. In order to produce clear logs, most of the branches of trees grown in Kitayama are cut off when small, leaving only a topknot of green to sustain the tree's growth. When they are felled, the bark is gently peeled off and the logs polished with special sand from a local river.

The finest lumber is usually found in the log's outer rings, where the tree has grown over the knots, but since logs are round, not square, cuts near the outside won't yield large timbers. These cuts are used for small-dimensioned pieces such as rafters or purlins, or for thin ceiling or finish roof boards. However, in old-growth trees in a closed-canopy forest, there isn't enough light to sustain the lower branches and they drop off early, before the trees grow into giants. From that point on clear lumber is made as the tree stretches toward the sunlight.

Incense cedar (*Calocedrus decurrens*, formerly known as *Libocedrus decurrens*). The guesthouse *tokonoma* pole, a prize piece of incense cedar, came from Brackett's own land. Slightly harder than Western red cedar, incense cedar heartwood has a pink or even orangish cast rather than the brown or tan characteristic of Western red cedar. It is also called "pencil cedar" since it is used to manufacture pencils, and it is virtually identical in wood quality to the Japanese *nezuko* (*Thuja standishii*). This cedar is a bit easier to work, and seems to be as rot resistant as Western red cedar, even if it is more prone to "checking" (carpenter's parlance for cracking) in the drying process. Brackett likes incense cedar, even more than Western red cedar, because of an endearing characteristic: if hand planed, it reflects artificial light

at night with a mirror-like sheen. When door panels are made of incense cedar, lights seem to dance on their surface.

Unlike Western red cedar, incense cedar trees have the drawback of retaining dead limbs, which attract fungal growth and can make the wood "pecky"—that is, full of chambers of dry rot. Finding large logs isn't too difficult, but finding large ones free from knots and peck is. When these logs become available, Brackett buys as many as he can, but sometimes he has to wait years for them to come along. Thirty years ago, Brackett began removing the lower limbs on many of the incense cedars on his own forest land. Now perfectly clear stems, free of visible knots, are growing there—ideal material for structural posts, *tokonoma* poles, or dramatic log beams. The trees are cut in the spring during a growth spurt, while their sap is running. At this time the bark is quite loose and if it is peeled off within hours of being felled, it can be removed without metal tools. The logs are then pressure washed to blast off their sugary sap, which could cause mold or discoloration. They are cut lengthwise to the center with one long cut so they can be wedged open and left to dry for a year or more. This cut, called *sewari* in Japanese, releases the inevitable tension that builds up as the log dries and leads to serious and random radial checking. By anticipating this problem the check is made intentionally wherever it is desired, leaving the rest of the log free of cracks. The log will then be used either as a beam with the *sewari* facing the ceiling or in a wall where it won't be seen.

Redwood (*Sequoia sempervirens*). Brackett formerly used redwood, but rarely does today because he prefers the color and flexibility of Western red cedar. The one exception is a series of boards given to him by Max Shaffrath, a physician in Sacramento, who came across an old-growth Sierra redwood that toppled over and died at Mountain Home State Park in the Sierras in 1992. These boards were cut at different levels: first at the base, where the diameter was 17 feet, and then 100 feet (10 stories) above the ground, where it was 12 feet. The smaller boards have about 2,450 annual rings; the larger, 2,550 rings, indicating that their growth started between 458 and 558 B.C. One of these radial cross sections made a memorable *ranma* (a transom above a sliding door head) in an East Wind house.

East Wind also stocks a large amount of redwood recycled from wine barrels made for Sebastiani Vineyards in 1906. They were dismantled in the 1980s, when most vineyards switched to stainless steel tanks. Some

Opposite page: The dark transom above this cabinet is made with wood from a cross section of a giant redwood more than 2,000 years old. Up close, all its rings can be counted, one by one, from the year the tree died, 1992, back to the year it reached 100 feet in height, 476 B.C. The cabinet, a modification of the traditional built-in, has a lower drawer that flips up so a futon can be slid in without lifting.

of this wine-stained wood was reborn as gable gratings, or *yagiri*, in the guesthouse.

PINES

In Japan pines, firs, and hemlocks are used in the traditional roof structure for their strength. Their relative lack of rot resistance isn't usually considered a problem, since this lumber won't get wet unless the roof leaks, and dry wood doesn't rot. Extraordinarily wide, clear boards might even be used in the *tokonoma*. Pines are commonly grouped according to the number of needles in a bundle, as two-needle pines, three-needle pines, and five-needle pines—the latter group all belonging to the white pine family.

Sugar pine, one of the five-needle or white pines, is another commonly used wood at East Wind, whose shop is in the middle of the best cluster of sugar pines in all of California. The sugar pine is the largest of the world's pine trees. The record holders are a tree 269.6 feet tall and another with a diameter of 18.13 feet. Examples of this enormous species, a favorite of the famous naturalist John Muir, stand alongside the old-growth sequoias in Yosemite National Park, and are so imposing that, were it not for their more famous neighbors, they would be the main attraction.

Sugar pine is gentle, sweet smelling (sugar actually builds up on the surface as it dries), yielding, and very easy on the tools—perhaps the most easily worked of all woods. Its heartwood and sapwood are almost indistinguishable until worked (the textures are different, even if their colors aren't). Sugar pine has a clear grain pattern with tiny little brown spots the size of ground pepper and conveys a gentle feeling. The fact that it is easy to plane indicates how well it behaves over the long run. It is also one of the most rot resistant of the pines. Of course no pine or fir demonstrates the rot resistance of the cedars, but sugar pine has been employed for years to make shakes and roofing in the Sierras, though it shouldn't be used too close to the ground or in damp areas.

Sugar pine is so stable—almost like plastic—that Mercedes and BMW used to buy the best available to use as pattern stock for wooden models of their components. Impressions were made from the models to produce castings for engine blocks and other parts. Only Honduran mahogany rivals sugar pine's stability and workability.

Opposite page: Ancient trees such as these rare, thousand-year-old redwoods in California produce fine-grained, clear lumber but at a high cost to the environment. East Wind opposes careless use of old-growth redwood.

Other pines. North America has dozens of species of pine, half of which are found in California and many of which are superb lumber trees. The long-leaf and short-leaf pines of the East Coast (*Pinus palustris* and *Pinus echinata*) and Eastern white pine (*Pinus strobus*) have all been used extensively for building. Eastern white pine, another five-needle pine, is almost white in color and bears a close resemblance to Port Orford cedar. East Wind was once given some small samples of foxtail pine (*Pinus balfouriana*) and bristlecone pine (*Pinus longaeva*). The latter species grows above ten thousand feet in the eastern Sierras and, as its scientific name suggests, includes the oldest living trees on earth, surpassing the oldest giant sequoia by fifteen hundred years. One particular bristlecone pine dubbed Methuselah has been documented as being more than forty-seven hundred years old. Brackett is saving his foxtail pine and bristlecone pine stock to use in a special way someday; their grain is so fine it is visible only with a magnifying glass. Each feels and looks more like coal than wood.

Brackett carefully allots his best lumber to buildings and parts of buildings where it will be fully appreciated. His staff reports that he occasionally says, "No, this is too good for this project." Nor will he use a post with four perfectly clear sides in a location where all four sides cannot be seen. Great care is taken to ensure that the clear faces of posts will be visible in the finished building, as well as to find locations where imperfect faces will be hidden. Using posts with four clear sides might entail less of a search through the stock of wood, but would be a waste of a rare material unless all four sides will be seen. "It isn't the cost," he says. "In fact, this adds to the cost. But that's all right. There are some things one doesn't do, because to do them is uncivilized. This kind of lumber is a treasure, and I would no more waste it than I would wipe my muddy feet on a Rembrandt painting. In my shop, we don't even step *over* wood, much less step *on* it. It never even touches the floor unless by accident, and we never throw away wood we can use for another project or in some other place."

Two other Western pines are noteworthy. The three-needle ponderosa pine (*Pinus ponderosa*) is the world's second-largest pine, and it, too, makes excellent lumber with a color ranging from pink to yellow. Ponderosa pine is a little harder than sugar pine, but not as strong as Douglas fir (*Pseudotsuga menziesii*). If sugar pine didn't exist, Japanese carpenters would talk about ponderosa pine with the same breathless affection they have for its sweeter relative. Western white pine (*Pinus monticola*), a five-needle pine, is usually larger than Eastern white pine, but Brackett has never had an opportunity to use it, although it is obviously very worthy.

Other carpenters use Douglas fir, a strong, readily available wood, but Brackett won't have it in his shop. He doesn't like its color or its grain, and he especially doesn't like working with it: "It's hard, cantankerous, difficult to work, dulls tools, and it's unstable and seems to bleed pitch forever." The Sierra Douglas fir is also too brittle, he finds.

OTHER WOODS

There are a variety of other woods at East Wind, simply because as Brackett says, "It's pretty hard for those who spend their lives looking at wood, thinking about wood, working with it, and making beautiful things of wood, to resist collecting it."

Wild cherry (*Prunus serratina*) is one of Brackett's favorites and, since it is not only beautiful but also very slippery, it was used in the guesthouse for the lower tracks (*shiki*) of the sliding wooden doors and shoji. Often overlooked because it is so common, wild cherry is a delight to work. It is of medium hardness, quite rot resistant, and hand planes to one of the finest finishes imaginable. When Port Orford cedar is used for *shiki*, cherry is inlaid into the track to give sliding doors the greatest ease of movement. Since wild cherry is harder than Port Orford cedar, the track will last longer too.

European elm (*Ulmus procera*) was employed in the large storage chest in the guesthouse that was designed to hold art prints and some hidden appliances (see photos on page 172). Both it and red elm (*Ulmus rubra*) closely resemble *keyaki*, or Japanese zelkova (*Zelkova serrata*), used there for structural posts and beams as well as for *tansu*. It is very hard wood, and East Wind uses it for *engawa* floorboards, sills, and pegs. Because of Dutch elm disease, all the elms, including red elm, are now nearly extinct in the United States. Most of East Wind's stock has come from Minnesota, where it was found through old family connections.

American chestnut (*Castanea dentate*) is Brackett's favorite hardwood, but he employs it guardedly, since it is even rarer than red elm. Of all the chestnuts (Japanese chestnut, Spanish chestnut, and others), it is certainly the best. As a lumber tree it is virtually extinct, except for isolated growth in the Sierras. The largest of the chestnut tribe, it was the biggest tree east of the Mississippi before a fungus decimated it in the early 1900s. By 1950, nine million acres of American chestnuts had been reduced to gray stumps. Brackett will do whatever he can to acquire chestnut except cut down a living tree. Recycled chestnut sometimes becomes available on the East Coast when old barns and houses are dismantled.

Chestnut is handsome, very rot resistant, and easy to work. It is used occasionally by East Wind for *tansu*, borders to bay windows, entryway sills, and around an open fire pit, since it resists heat well. Recognizing its stability, the Japanese use chestnut for temple railings (*koran*), which must endure the elements unprotected. The lumber ages to the rich, warm reddish brown color of roasted chestnuts and, for a hardwood, is quite soft.

Fortunately, American chestnut may soon reappear in quantity thanks to years of determined efforts by plant geneticists and plant pathologists in Minnesota and Virginia, who have dedicated their lives to selective breeding of a blight-resistant species. If they are successful, it will be a great gift to the American continent, since the trees not only improve forest diversity and provide beautiful lumber but also produce large crops of chestnuts that are an important food for many wildlife species.

Myrtle (also known as California laurel, *Umbellularia californica*) is also used for *tokonoma* boards and other decorative applications such as *tansu* and other furniture. With its very strong bay-leaf scent, this tree is different from *Laurus nobilis*, the traditional laurel of the Mediterranean. The heartwood can be either spectacular or rather nondescript.

California nutmeg (*Torreya californica*) is used sparingly for finish interior floor sills and occasionally for tables. It has a reputation for "correcting" dents made in it and it also makes a characteristic sound, which is why it is the preferred material for making boards for the game *go*, in which stones are slapped onto the board with a distinctive sound.

Black and English walnut (*Juglans nigra* and *Juglans regia*), most of it a gift from Phelps, is also stocked by East Wind for step-up boards, *tokonoma*, and occasionally for *tansu*. All the walnuts are known for their relative softness (for a hardwood), their stability, attractive grain, and rich colors, which is why they have been a favorite wood for furniture manufacturing for centuries.

Camphor (*Cinnamomum camphora*). Brackett finds camphor logs from time to time, usually in the Sacramento Valley, where it is a common street tree. With a strong, medicinal, antiseptic smell, camphor is the traditional choice

A step in the entryway is the signal to shed shoes. This step-up board (*fumi ita*) is made of a single English walnut plank chosen for its particular grain pattern and color.

for lavatory vanity tops and toilet floors. In fact, its fumes are so intense that they can sicken woodworkers when it is being milled and worked.

California black oak (*Quercus kellogi*) on Brackett's property becomes cabinet tops and, occasionally, wide plank floors. Common in the Sierra foothills, it belongs to the red oak family. It has a pretty brown color very similar to English oak, is quite soft for an oak, relatively stable, and can grow to be gigantic.

Pacific yew (*Taxus brevifolia*) was put aside for the *hikite*, the finger pulls in doors and windows, and for other places where its rich, dark, multicolored grain would be appreciated. An extremely hard wood, it is the preferred material for long bows. Pacific yew grows very slowly, sometimes increasing only an inch of diameter in a century.

In Brackett's home, California black oak from his land has been turned into wide plank flooring. The table, also made at East Wind, is cherry, with a hand-rubbed finish. An open fire is made in the fire pit with extremely dry, local oak. The room's wooden doors are removed in summer.

Maki (*Podocarpus macrophyllus*), is native to Japan and China. Its very fragrant, soft, blonde wood is prized for bathtubs for its pleasant scent and rot resistance.

Sitka spruce (*Picea sitchenis*), the largest of the spruce family, is a very strong wood but light in weight, with little scent. Its strength-to-weight ratio made it ideal for airplanes, and it was declared a "strategic material" during World War II. One of its primary roles today is in making soundboards for pianos and guitar faces. In the construction of Japanese houses, it is the second choice after members of the *hinoki* family for posts, perimeter beams, and so forth. East Wind generally avoids it, since it isn't particularly rot-resistant, is somewhat unstable, and doesn't have a very remarkable grain pattern.

East Wind's lumber rarely comes from retail yards, but from loggers and small, trusted sawmills up and down the West Coast. Some of Brackett's acquisitions are stories in themselves. For example, the sugar pine used in the guesthouse, which has been curing in the builder's yard for almost twenty years, originated with a phone call from a logger, Dennis Eliot. Following Eliot's instructions, Brackett headed south through the Sierras, traveling through the northernmost stand of giant sequoias and climbing higher to arrive at French Meadows. There he saw a "blow down," a swath of destruction one hundred to three hundred yards wide and about a mile long. There were two-hundred-forty-foot sugar pines, still alive, with three-story-high root balls, their tops twenty feet off the ground, but they were all doomed. Every tree was uprooted, tops pointing up the mountain.

Dennis handed Len a spray can, and told him to "take the tenderloin"— to mark cut lines with his initials in any tree he wanted before the lot was sold off to the local mill. (In those days the harvesting restraint rules were much looser than they are today, particularly those concerned with blow downs or salvage timber operations. Today, the Forest Service might very well prohibit taking such trees.) Three log trucks were loaded, all of them over the weight limit with the most splendid sugar pine Brackett had ever seen. The species, like redwood, can hold a lot of water, so logs are very heavy even though the dry lumber is relatively lightweight.

One truck could carry only two thirty-three-foot logs; one held three logs and one had four. Each truck weighed more than forty tons loaded. The logs were so heavy that even sizeable loaders couldn't lift them, much less move them onto a small sawmill. So in the July sun Brackett and his friend Walter Hardzog roughly quartered them with a chain saw. (It had a very large powerhead at either end of an eight-foot bar.) Later Brackett prevailed upon a local mill that had a log splitter to let him place the giant logs on a bunk under a steel track supporting a twelve-foot electric chain saw. The logs came out precisely quartered, but even then were barely moveable. After milling, the lumber was set aside and allowed to dry two to five years before it was selected, one piece at a time, for a specific use in an East Wind house. Most of it was clear, perfect lumber. Even better, it was all salvage!

Several years later, an impulse resulted in another kind of windfall. Brackett was driving home in his ten-wheeler flatbed when the head gasket began to blow *again*. All he could think of was how much he hated having a big truck, and wouldn't it be great if he could just get rid of the damned

Measuring Wood

A board foot, a measure of wood volume, is a piece of wood one inch thick, twelve inches wide, and one foot long. To compute board feet, multiply thickness (in inches) by width (in inches) by length (in feet) by number of pieces and divide by twelve.

The formula is:
number of pieces x thickness (inches) x width (inches) x length (feet) ÷ 12 = number of board feet

Japan measures in cubic meters today, but its traditional carpenters have a system of measure called *koku,* which is similar to board feet. One *koku* is a piece of wood one *shaku* (one foot) thick by one *shaku* wide by ten *shaku* long.

One koku = 120 board feet

thing. So he called Skyler Phelps and asked him if he wanted a truck. "You mean your ten-wheeler that can carry forty-eight thousand pounds?" "Yes, the same. Want to buy it?"

Phelps assured him a deal was probably in the making and suggested he bring it in, which Brackett was happy to do, since one of the reasons he'd called him in the first place was that he was nearby and didn't want to drive the thing the rest of the way home.

When he arrived in his friend's yard there was a truck fully loaded with a type of log he had never seen before. Phelps said that they were California nutmeg, and that an international lumber broker was eager to have them since the Japanese thought highly of them. Brackett took out his pocketknife and whittled a piece that had split off a log. He liked the way it cut, could see it had possibilities, and on the spot offered the hated truck to Phelps for the load. The trade was made. It wasn't until later that they found out the logs were what Brackett knew as *kaya* in Japan, worth a fortune. By then, East Wind had milled the smaller and knottier lower-grade logs and sunk the butt logs (the lower end of the trunk) in a friend's pond, where they stayed for the next fifteen years safely preserved without danger of drying out and checking.

In 1999 the neighbor needed to dredge the pond, pulled out the logs, and called Brackett to remove them. Brackett realized that unless he did something with them quickly, he would have logs so badly checked that anything milled would already be full of checks (cracks) and be unuseable. He wasn't interested in selling them to the Japanese market—

Doyle's Rule

Since the milling of a log entails considerable effort, it is worth knowing in advance how much lumber a given log might produce. Doyle's Rule gives a rough idea quickly.

Look at the smaller end of a 16-foot log. Measure its diameter inside the bark in inches. If it's an irregular circle, use the average of the longest and shortest diameters. Subtract 4 from the diameter and square the result. This number is the board feet that can be taken from a 16-foot log. The formula can be expressed as follows:

$$BF \text{ (for a 16-foot log)} = (D - 4)^2$$

Example: A 16-foot log with a diameter (smaller end) of 24 inches:
$(24 - 4) \times (24 - 4) = 400$ board feet

Logs of other lengths can be estimated based on the calculation for a 16-foot log. A 12-foot log, for example, will have three-quarters of the board footage of a 16-foot log. The shape of the log—tapered or straight—will, of course, affect the precise yield, but the formula is a handy, if rough, rule of thumb.

because he takes a very dim view of log exporters—so he had them milled into a stunning set of matched, clear, pale yellow lumber that the Japanese would have been amazed to see, though Americans generally don't even recognize it as special. Most of the lumber is still sitting at East Wind waiting for Americans to catch up with Japanese connoisseurship and discover its quality.

On another occasion, Brackett found himself over his head in a bidding war with the giant Sumitomo Company for a single log of Western red cedar. To his surprise, he emerged victorious. His biggest bargain over the years? He once paid two hundred dollars for a two-hundred-five-foot sugar pine sold as salvage, which yielded an astronomical 12,500 board feet.

East Wind's most reliable sources for quality lumber are the two mills in Oregon and Canada to which he turned for the guesthouse. Often the milling process is initiated with no more than a conversation, and the price is worked out later. Other times a logger will refer Brackett to someone who has specific logs, which Brackett goes to see. The curved log beam of incense cedar chosen to span the cottage art gallery came from a local logger during a National Forest timber sale. A sizeable parcel of land was being logged to thin out the stand—a common practice in that area of the Sierras, where the problem isn't getting the trees to grow but trying to keep too many from growing in the same spot. These trees had bent trunks.

Loggers and sawmills tend to avoid such logs, since it is hard to get straight lumber out of a bent log, but East Wind likes to use them to arch across a room as an exposed beam.

The only time East Wind ever bought logs without prior inspection was a disaster. Although an explanation of how to buy a log and what to look for is beyond the scope of this book, Brackett has one bit of advice: "Don't ever buy logs over the phone. Look at them first, or if you don't know what you're looking at, find someone who'll tell you the truth and who will help. Above all, don't let a logger or its owner tell you how great a log is!"

Large pieces free of defects, knots, check, or rot are always the rarest. Clear 2 x 4s are fairly common, especially if they're short, but long, perfect 6 x 12s are very rare. Even when large logs that appear to be fine are found, they remain a mystery until milling reveals what's inside. Logs that show great promise can be great disappointments. Knots, check, spiral grain, and rot can appear when least expected, dashing hopes. "On the other hand," Brackett says, "a ratty log can sometimes produce splendid lumber, so buying logs is somewhat of a crap shoot." Because of this uncertainty, Brackett normally works with the mill, watching as the inside of the log is exposed and directing how it can be milled to its best advantage for his current project.

MILLING

The milling operation is usually concentrated on producing specific components from specific woods, such as ceiling boards from Western red cedar or posts from Port Orford cedar or timbers from sugar pine. After a quarter length of the log has been cut, it is turned ninety degrees; the suspense mounts as all await what the new cuts will reveal. The entire process can take many anxiety-fraught hours. Clear, beautifully colored, perfect lumber appears to triumphant high-fives, but a great spiraling check is a crushing defeat. There's always the risk that a very valuable log doesn't pan out. This is why fine lumber is rare, and why Brackett can't stand to see it wasted.

The Canadian mill mentioned earlier is operated by a family that emigrated from Taiwan three generations ago. Before settling in Canada, they had milled cypress and cedar for Kyoto's temples—the most technically demanding traditional architecture in Japan—for a century. At their first meeting, the mill owner showed Brackett photo albums of work he and his family had done—among them, serendipitously, was a build-

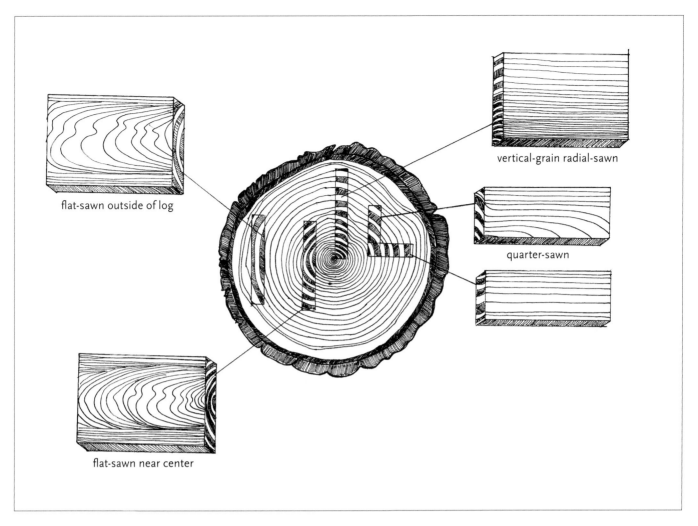

flat-sawn outside of log

vertical-grain radial-sawn

quarter-sawn

flat-sawn near center

This drawing illustrates how a log can be milled to produce different types of grain patterns. Drawing by Aya Brackett.

ing in Kyoto on which Brackett had worked during his apprenticeship. It was part of Tenryuji, one of the larger Zen temples in Kyoto; Brackett and another carpenter had done the layout for a very complex roof on a covered walkway there.

Both of the mills that supply East Wind know just how to mill the different species found in their locales. Canada produces Western red cedar, Alaskan yellow cedar, and Sitka spruce. Oregon raises Port Orford cedar, incense cedar, sugar pine, Sitka spruce, and Pacific yew. California is rich in sugar pine, incense cedar, some Port Orford cedar, black oak, American chestnut, ponderosa pine, California nutmeg, walnut, camphor, and a host of other woods. The mills are generally given identification numbers to attach to each piece that indicate its function (rafters, posts, beams, and so forth), finish dimension, number of faces free of defect, species, and the amount of material that can be removed in the planing process to bring it to finish dimension.

Boards are cut out of the length of the log in three basic ways: flat-sawn, vertical-sawn, or quarter-sawn, each producing a distinct grain. The

Seen from inside, the matched flat grain of Western red cedar roof boards becomes a design element in the guesthouse, where structure is the décor. The naturally curved incense cedar log supports the roof loads.

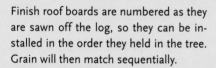

Finish roof boards are numbered as they are sawn off the log, so they can be installed in the order they held in the tree. Grain will then match sequentially.

Three perfect, sixteen-inch, matched flat-grain, old-growth Western red cedar boards are placed side by side. Such boards are generally used for dropped ceilings that conceal roof structure. Being lower, they can be more readily seen and appreciated.

Japanese language has terms not only for these three different grains but also words for fine distinctions within each of the three. "Bamboo-shoot" grain (takenoko moku), for example, or "jewel grain" (tama moku) describe specific grain patterns within flat-sawn lumber, both of which are highly prized in Japan.

Flat-sawn

Flat-sawn boards have flame patterns on their face and arc patterns on their end grain. In the guesthouse, they were chosen to enrich the visual appeal of the exposed roof structure, the dropped ceilings, and the door panels. Flat-sawn boards are cut at a right angle to the radius of the log, in other words, on the tangent, which is why the grain is sometimes called tangential. These boards are also called flat-grain or plain-sawn, and are the easiest kind to mill, since the log doesn't have to be rotated frequently as it does in the production of either radial or quarter-sawn grain.

Ceiling boards require very specific milling procedures to produce boards with this highly prized grain pattern. The flat-grain pattern should run up the middle of the board's face. The grain of a wide, flat-grain board will tend to become more vertical towards the edges, so care has to be taken to have the pattern balanced on each board. Ideally the boards should be coded with three numbers as they come off the log: the first is a number assigned to the log, the second is the face of that log, and the third is the number of the board taken from that face. The coding 3-4-6, for example, indicates the third log, fourth face cut on that log, sixth board cut from that face. Usually there are four sawn faces in a log when it is milled for flat-grained lumber. First one face is cut and then the log is "turned" ninety degrees, placing the sawn face down, and another face is started. Each face will produce a series of successive boards.

The flame patterns of this grain should always be installed in the building pointing up, the way the tree grows. Any other orientation will strike the careful carpenter as a violation of the natural upright character of the tree. (Experienced woodworkers can identify the front, back, top and bottom of a board by looking at it.) In Japan, such sakasama (upside-down) boards are regarded as bad luck. Brackett doesn't subscribe to this superstition, but he still doesn't like seeing an upside-down installation. "Perhaps the bad luck really stems," he suggests, "from the fact that a carpenter who installs boards upside down isn't paying attention to his work."

There is also a superstition about the proper installation of horizontal wood grain: if it is placed, let us say, in the panels of adjoining wooden

In Japan skilled carpenters try to place a flat-sawn board the way it grew, root end down, growing end up. The "flame tips" in the grain pattern are the telltale sign. They are correct on these sliding doors.

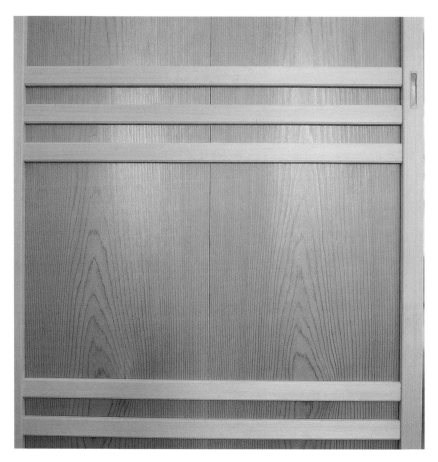

sliding doors, butt to butt (root end to root end), and not head to head, the homeowners will divorce. Like most Japanese carpenters today, Brackett finds this precaution amusing, but some Japanese carpenters are still careful to avoid this.

The grain of the side of a flat-sawn board closest to bark of the tree is called *omote me*, or front grain, and the side facing the interior is the *ura me*, or back grain. In most applications, the front grain is preferable to the back grain because it displays its growth rings in a wider arc. Outside grain is also starker, more striking, and is usually the preferred exposed face. And as we saw before, it is less likely to have knots. To determine the front from the back, one simply looks at the end grain: the top of the arc points towards the front face. You can also run your hand along a face from the top of the "flame tips" to the bottom. If it feels smooth—that is, if there's no chance of catching a splinter—then that's the outside. You are quite likely to get splinters if you run your hand along the inside.

As a tree adds a ring of new growth over the previous year's growth, it becomes an elongated cone, wide at the bottom and narrow at the top. If it is milled into boards with saw cuts more or less parallel to the center of the log, then the structure of a board or a timber becomes more understandable. Starting at the top-of-the-tree end of the board, the layers are laid down over the layers closer to the root of the tree, the bottom of the board. Try several times to determine the front from the back and then check the verdict with a look at the end grain. It will soon be possible to identify front and back without touching the lumber.

The ability to do this has a practical application. The back of a flat-grain board usually, but not always, becomes convex when it dries, while the front becomes concave. Placing the back side out would be useful, for example, in exterior siding, since as the board dries its edge pushes down on the board it overlaps and holds it tightly in place. In most cases, though, the outside of the board is preferred, and it is usually the face visible in a Japanese house.

Vertical-sawn

Vertical-sawn, the least dramatic of the three cuts, is recognized by its tight parallel lines and plain appearance. These boards, also called radially-sawn or rift-sawn, are cut *along* the radius of the log. Since they are the most stable—the least likely to warp or shrink— they were the best choice for the guesthouse bathtub and for its woven ceiling.

Most Japanese carpenters like to use this quiet vertical grain in places where visual restraint or the cut's inherent stability is needed. In addition to bathtubs, such locations include some floors, wall paneling, or places where the finish roof boards are visible from below. If the visible roof structure is complex, the added complexity of flat grain is more distracting than calming. Roof boards shouldn't compete with the structural complexity of the roof for attention. Brackett wasn't aware of this when he built his own house, which has a complex exposed roof structure. The dominant grain patterns of the flat-grain redwood he used for its lean-to roofs are confusing and difficult to see, being transected constantly with valleys, battens, and rafters. Only when he used vertical grain for the last lean-to roofs around his central garden did he realize it was a better choice.

All wood has lateral rays of cells that extend from the pith in the center of the tree out through the heartwood and the sapwood into the bark, where they are called phloem rays. (Phloem is a vascular tissue that conducts sucrose solution throughout the tree.) Running parallel to the radius in bands that are scarcely visible, their width varies from species to species. However, some woods, such as sycamore and certain oaks, have pronounced rays. These woods are intentionally rift-sawn—sawn right down or very near the radius of the log—to produce wood showing these spectacular flecks. Even though these rays are hard to see in other softwoods, they make their presence known because of the difficulty encountered in finish planing them well.

Quarter-sawn

Quarter-sawn is between flat-sawn and vertical-sawn and partakes of the characteristics of both. First the log is quartered lengthwise, and then cuts are made down the two flat faces of each quarter. The cuts start more or less at the radius and move away from it with each cut. To do this best, a number of cuts will be made from one face of the log, and then the log is rolled over ninety degrees to expose the other face for cutting. Quarter- sawing lumber is more expensive, since the quarter log has to be turned repeatedly, which adds to the milling cost. Most of the cuts look vertical-sawn until the other face being cut is approached and the lumber begins to increasingly resemble flat-sawn. Even though cuts are made along the same axis, the last slices are at a right angle to the radius and are flat-sawn. (See drawing on page 77).

Logs cut this way are quite stable in response to changes in humidity. The lumber for many of the posts and door components in the guesthouse were quarter-sawn to ensure stability. The window-frame materials were cut so their faces are either vertical or quarter grain to prevent warpage into or out of the plane of the opening. Side to side warpage of door stiles is usually precluded because the horizontal frame members (rails) tie the verticals (stiles) together.

DRYING WOOD

Lumber must be fully dried before working it or it will continue to shrink, warp, and check afterwards. Larger posts and timbers take a long time to dry, so forethought and planning are necessary if one wants to use cured, dry lumber.

After cutting, lumber is dried outdoors at East Wind for as long as five years, protected from rain and sun under sheet metal canopies. Once dry, lumber must be *kept* dry. If it gets wet, the drying process has been a waste of time and it is no better than green lumber. For twenty years Brackett has been stockpiling and drying lumber this way. He is probably one of the last builders to do this anywhere, even in Japan He now keeps a two-acre inventory of approximately two hundred thousand board feet in ten-foot high piles, and it was this supply that provided much of the lumber for the guesthouse.

Since lumber dries faster at the ends, the ends are waxed using Anchor Seal, a water-based paraffin paint, to prevent them from drying too fast, which leads to checking. When the water evaporates after application, only a soft paraffin remains which seals the end grain. Markings on ends indicate defect-free faces.

Wooden strips from $^1/_4$ to $1^1/_2$ inches thick, called "stickers," are inserted into the lumber layers to allow moderate air circulation. Ideally, stickers should not be made of pine or any other lumber that tends to "blue"—becomes discolored due to mildew or mold growth—because blue stripes will appear on the lumber. Conscientious mills usually use stickers of white fir, Port Orford, or red or incense cedar.

Sometimes the lumber unit is covered with a plastic sheet under a tin roof to further slow air exchange. This is advisable to prevent damage to valuable or large pieces during hot, dry weather, especially when the lumber is freshly cut and very wet. Plastic should not be used as its sole protection, however, since it inevitably degrades and cracks in the sunlight and is nearly impossible to keep in place in high winds. Also, plastic sheeting conforms to the contours of the pile, allowing the formation of pools that collect water, which inevitably sink between the pieces of lumber and finally rupture. This soaks everything inside and cuts off air circulation, creating a perfect environment for mildew, mold, discoloration, and finally rot.

If lumber is dried too rapidly, it can check. As the skin shrinks and stretches over the still wet, nonshrinking core, stresses build up until a portion of the wood gives. Large pieces of lumber can check badly. Using smaller stickers helps slow the process by reducing air circulation.

Moisture evaporates fastest from the ends of sawn lumber. As the ends dry, they begin to shrink. Since the interior is still moist, "end checking" appears and runs deeper and deeper into the lumber as the whole piece dries. However, if the ends of stored lumber are sealed with, for example,

Calculating Dimensional Changes in Drying Wood

In order to know how much wood will expand or contract in different applications one must first know its present moisture content and its future moisture content. There are three ways to determine what the moisture content (equilibrium moisture content or EMC) of wood will be when installed in a given location.

The first way is to simply use a wood moisture meter to measure wood that's been in the location for a period of time. This is the easiest. The second is to measure the average relative humidity of the air at that location, and from that figure, calculate future equilibrium moisture content. Dividing the average relative humidity by 5 will more or less tell what its moisture content will be in that environment.

The third way involves using moisture tables in a wood handbook, which will provide exact equilibrium moisture contents versus relative humidities. Finding the difference between the wood's expected equilibrium moisture content and its current moisture content gives one the first figure to use in the calculation.

This difference in moisture content (4% in the example below) is compared to the range where moisture content changes results in dimensional change. We know that as wood gets wetter, dimensional change stops when the moisture content gets as high as 25% to 30% (an average of 27.5%), and that as wood dries once all water is gone (0% moisture content), no further dimensional change occurs.

Let's say the wood is going from 16% moisture content to 12%, a change of 4%. Divide the change, 4%, by 27.5% (the range where moisture content makes any difference) and then multiply by the percent of dimensional change characteristic of the particular species and the particular cut, according to the chart on the opposite page. Multiply again by the dimension of the face under consideration. The resulting number will tell you how much the wood will expand or contract.

The formula for an 8-inch wide, flat-sawn, sugar pine board would be:

0.04 divided by .275 x .056 (sugar pine flat grain movement) x 8 inches (width of board) = 0.06516 inches (about 1/16 of an inch:the amount of expected movement, larger or smaller whichever is the case)

Some of this lumber will take up to five years to dry before it's ready to use, some less. Thin strips of wood called "stickers" are placed between the layers to permit air circulation. Modern technology now allows lumber to be dried in a few days in a radio-frequency oven.

This table presents average shrinkage values, from green to oven dry, for some of the species commonly used by East Wind. (Douglas fir is included because many use it, although East Wind doesn't.) Softwoods tend to be slightly more stable than hardwoods.

Hardwoods

Species	Percent radial shrinkage	Percent tangential shrinkage
Black cherry	3.7	7.1
American elm	4.2	9.5
Slippery elm (red elm)	4.9	8.9
Black walnut	5.5	7.8
Big leaf maple	3.7	7.1
American chestnut	3.4	6.7
English (European) walnut	4.5	6.8
Black oak	4.4	11.1
Sassafras	4.2	6.6

Softwoods

Species	Percent radial shrinkage	Percent tangential shrinkage
Alaska yellow cedar	2.8	6.0
Incense cedar	3.3	5.2
Port Orford cedar	4.6	6.9
Western red cedar	2.4	5.0
Ponderosa pine	3.9	6.2
Sugar pine	2.9	5.6
Douglas fir, coast	4.8	7.6
Douglas fir, interior West	4.8	7.5
Redwood, old growth	2.6	4.4
Redwood, young growth	2.2	4.9
Sitka spruce	4.3	7.5

Source: Forest Products Laboratory, US Forest Service, Madison, Wisconsin
**Coast Douglas Fir is defined as Douglas fir growing in Oregon and Washington west of the summit of the Cascade Mountains. Interior West includes California and all counties in Oregon and Washington east of but adjacent to the Cascade summit.

paint or paraffin (the latter available emulsified in a water base), most of the moisture has to escape from the sides, and the ends will dry at more or less the same rate as the rest, reducing the likelihood of end checking. The sealant is removed when the lumber is worked.

Some woods are more stable than others. It has been Brackett's experience that softer woods are usually more stable than harder ones. The most stable American softwoods are Western red cedar, redwood, and sugar pine. Soft "hardwoods" like Honduran mahogany and paulownia (*Paulownia tomentosa*) are also quite stable, as are chestnut and sassafras. Some of the very dense hardwoods such as hickory and many of the oaks are very unstable and continue to contract and expand even when dry.

"Dry" is always a relative term when applied to wood, which contains water in two forms: free water, which will literally squirt you in the eye, and water that is chemically bound up. Lumber does not begin to change shape or shrink until the free water is gone and the lumber no longer feels wet, which means the moisture content is down to about twenty-five to thirty percent. Only at that point does the water within the cells begin to evaporate and changes in the wood's shape start to occur.

The moisture content (as a percentage of weight) will be higher for a given piece of wood when the atmospheric humidity is higher. The damper the air, the wetter the wood. Wood is considered dry when "equilibrium moisture content" is achieved, that is, it is neither accepting nor losing moisture. At the end of the relatively wet winter, the dry lumber in Brackett's yard has a moisture content of about twelve percent, and at the end of the sunny, hot, dry California summer, about ten percent. Both measures are at equilibrium with the prevailing humidity of the season, and the lumber won't get any drier no matter how long it's left out. Wood dries to zero percent moisture only in an oven or kiln, but in that state it will reabsorb atmospheric moisture as soon as it is exposed to it.

Wood expands and shrinks according to its species (see chart on page 85) as well as the relative humidity of its environment. Generally, its moisture content will be about one-fifth the percentage of relative humidity. (Atmospheric humidity in this case refers to the average relative humidity over a twenty-four-hour period, not just the hygrometer reading at a particular moment.) The larger the piece of wood, the longer it takes to come to equilibrium with the water content of the air around it. This time period can range from a couple of days for a small piece of lumber to years for large timbers or posts.

Any species will shrink more or less twice as much tangentially as radially, which means that if shrinkage and warping are a concern, vertical grain will always be the most reliable no matter what the species. The percentage of movement shown in the chart represents an average of many samples for that species, so the percentages are generally accurate but not absolutely precise, because each tree is an *individual*.

Some woods, particularly redwood and sugar pine, hold vast amounts of water. Their weight when wet can be twice that when dried. (Loggers call such logs "sinkers," since they are so wet they won't even float.) The amount of water in a freshly cut log is also affected by the season in which it's cut. Logs are drier in winter when the sap is in the roots and wettest in spring when new growth occurs. A common rule is that each inch of thickness takes a year to air dry. This can be misleading. Lumber will dry much quicker in a place like California in the summer, which is quite dry (has a low relative humidity) than on the East Coast of the United States, where the relative humidity is high in summer. Softwoods seem to dry quicker than hardwoods. Brackett finds that sugar pine timbers dry in two to four years in California, which is considerably less than what is considered necessary elsewhere.

The trick, Brackett says, is to predict how much water the wood will absorb or lose later under varying conditions—that is, how much the wood will expand or shrink—and to take this value into account when using it in a building. Ignorance or bad judgment about where the wood will be used, or lack of knowledge of its present moisture content can lead to cracks in doors and ceilings, drawers that lock shut in high humidity, joints that come apart, and multiple other problems.

With very stable woods, the shrinkage or expansion of vertical grain from oven dry to soaking wet can be as low as 2.5 percent for vertical-sawn lumber as compared to 5 percent for flat-sawn lumber. For some hardwoods these percentages can be double-digit numbers. Longitudinal shrinkage is minimal, changing about 0.1 percent from soaking wet to oven dry.

KILNS AND RADIO-FREQUENCY VACUUM KILNS

Kiln drying, which greatly speeds the drying process, as opposed to air drying, also has its place in this kind of construction. There are many types of kilns, operating at different rates of speed and causing differing degrees of damage to the lumber. Some species like Port Orford cedar, Douglas fir, pines, and many of the hardwoods respond well to kiln drying. The species that don't do well, like Western red cedar, redwood, and incense cedar, have wood structures that seem much more vulnerable to the degrading effects of kilns. These woods shouldn't be kiln dried, but if they are, then great care must be used, and very specific methods are necessary to avoid completely ruining a kiln load. Grain collapse can result, or the plasticity and resilience of the wood can be seriously compromised (a condition described as "brash" or "brashiness"). Grain collapse results in large hollow pockets, internal checking, and lumber that loses its structural integrity. "Brash" is very apparent when hand or machine planing. The shavings of the hand plane fall apart, and dust instead of curls emerge from the machine plane. Such wood is brittle, crumbly, without life or sheen.

Standard commercial kilns cannot accommodate the long, slow process necessary to properly dry the large and expensive timbers and posts that are employed in Japanese architecture. Large lumber requires drying at a very low temperature over a long period of time, and kilns need to concentrate on the high-heat, high-volume business of their bread-and-butter customers who need standard framing materials such as 2 x 4s, 2 x 6s, and 2 x 8s.

Recently, however, a new technology called radio-frequency vacuum drying (RFV) has reduced the drying time from several years to an extraordinary four to six days. RFV uses an enormous vacuum chamber to "microwave" lumber in a twofold process. The vacuum in the chamber reduces the relative humidity to near zero, which allows moisture to escape from the lumber very rapidly. At the same time, the microwave heats the interior of the lumber and can even boil it, especially in the vacuum, which forces the water out the ends. It also, of course, heats the lumber, accelerating the drying. Drying is faster in heat than in cold because the activity of water molecules accelerates with heat environment.

An RFV kiln uses enormous amounts of electricity, however, and the cost is significant. Increased transportation costs are involved as well, since such kilns are almost always located in a remote location where electricity rates are low. The lumber has to travel from the sawmill to the RFV kiln and then to East Wind. Kilns available for use on the West Coast are found in British Columbia, a considerable distance from most of the mills East Wind uses.

A benefit of the RFV kiln is that it precludes the need to keep a huge inventory of timbers on hand: only the lumber needed for the building being constructed needs to be prepared. Considerable capital is needed to acquire and store large inventories, and this is a business cost that ultimately affects the cost of the house. In addition, while stored inventories offer many advantages, they also need constant care and protection from the elements, and they are almost always made without a specific building in mind, based on speculation that the lumber will eventually be used in some project. Another problem with an inventory of dry lumber is that if smaller timbers are required but aren't on hand, then large timbers must be resawn, which results in considerable mill scrap, a great waste of this precious material. It would be far less wasteful to mill the smaller timber from logs and to dry them immediately. Additionally, in the air-drying process a certain percentage of the lumber will be unavoidably degraded through checking, blue stain, or other discoloration; the kiln-drying process makes this less likely.

The RFV kiln also saves time in the building process, since all the lumber needed for a building is in one place, eliminating days of labor going through and pulling lumber out of storage. Even though transportation of the lumber to the RFV kiln may be more expensive, capital investment expense is considerably reduced, less lumber has to be used, and waste is significantly reduced. Still, the old-fashioned method of selecting the lumber one piece at a time, while it is more labor intensive (and may cost more than the lumber itself), it is sometimes the only way to arrive at quality work.

When all the dry lumber was selected for the guesthouse, work could begin in earnest, transforming the raw materials into the many different components that make a house. The next chapter examines that astonishingly precise process.

The three sacred marking tools of traditional Japanese carpentry, the square, bamboo pen, and inkline, are displayed in Shinto shrines dedicated to carpentry.

4 JOINERY

WITH THE KIND OF WOOD FOR each component determined, the next step is to select dry lumber from the yard inventory and add it to what had been specially milled and RFV kiln-dried for the project. Using properly cured lumber is the only way to ensure that a building will look as good in ten years as the day it was completed. The quality and style of the guesthouse were considered in the choice of the lumber, along with the function of each part and its specific location in the structure. First each component was processed on a large band saw, an apparatus so big it has its own concrete foundation. Then each was straightened and squared on two adjacent faces with a 20-inch jointer. Finally each component was sized to the exact dimensions required with a dimensional planer, using the already straight and square faces as a reference.

LAYOUT OF JOINTS

The *toryo* (head carpenter) then began the critical layout process, precisely drawing the cut lines for the joints on the lumber. Layout is considered the carpenter's most difficult task. For the guesthouse it was done principally by Ryosei Kaneko and James Wiester under Brackett's supervision. The markings were drawn in ink using a square (*sashigane*), a bamboo pen (*sumisashi*), and an inkpot and snap line (*sumitsubo*), the three sacred instruments sometimes seen in Shinto shrines dedicated to carpentry. The bamboo pen draws a fine, jet-black line for tens of feet with just one dip into the ink. This ink, *sumi*, is essentially the same used in Japanese ink paintings, or *sumi-e*. It saturates a bundle of raw silk in the vessel that soaks the snap line drawn through it. It is important that these black lines, snapped or drawn, not rub or wash off. Unlike a felt-tipped marker, the ink doesn't penetrate the wood deeply and can be easily planed off when the joint is cut. It is far better than a pencil, which will rub off, isn't very black or very visible, and which also scores the wood even if its marks are planed off.

Carpenters are always on the lookout for bamboo to make their pens. Bamboo over five years old is very hard and will hold a sharp edge for a long time. (Aged bamboo is so hard it can be made into nails that will penetrate oak.) The bamboo is split from the culm and then shaped and immersed in water for a couple of hours to hydrate its structure and make it easier to work. When it is saturated, multiple splits are easily made with a chisel, extending the cracks into the pen approximately an inch and a quarter about every $1/32$ or $1/64$ of an inch. The end now has lots of little flaps that enable the ink to flow smoothly to the end. Finally the end is shaped with a chisel into a beveled edge. (See photo on page 90.)

If the other end of the bamboo is pulverized with a hammer and dipped into ink, it can be used like a felt-tipped marker to assign location coding or make other layout marks on lumber. After several months of use and repeated re-cutting to resharpen it, the *sumisashi* is discarded and another is made to replace it.

JOINTS

One of the most intriguing features of classic Japanese architecture is that its buildings are held together by joinery. Techniques elaborately refined since the eighth century produce structures with some of the most sophisticated joinery in the world. The constructions are not only extremely strong, they result in very clean, precise work. The wood components are cut to interlock perfectly without nails.

The various joints used for the guesthouse were dictated by their location or their purpose. They had to be absolutely accurate or they would have little strength; a loose joint is useless if not dangerous, and of course they had to be made in the right place or the building wouldn't work at all.

There are two main classes of joinery: joints used to connect lumber at an angle (usually ninety degrees) and those used to join two or more pieces end to end to make one long one, which are sometimes known as "scarf joints."

In the guesthouse, every timber that connects with another to form an "L" or a "T" required a right-angle joint. It was used, therefore, at all corners and for joints between perimeter beams (keta) and posts, and between keta and all transverse beams, and between sills and posts.[1] It also was called on in the construction of the doors, although in a much smaller form.

The two most common joints in any Japanese house are the mortise-and-tenon joint and the dovetail. Both have myriad variations that have developed over the years. Some have been altered for visual reasons; others have been created to accommodate special loads; and still others function to borrow structural support from an adjacent component.

Mortise and Tenon One of the oldest joints, the versatile mortise-and-tenon joint is found in all woodworking cultures. A tenon is a projection from a timber or post that fits very tightly into a cavity or mortise cut into another piece. For a usual size post-to-keta connection, the standard East Wind tenon is about 1.25 inches thick, and its width is about 1 inch less than the total width of the post. The length varies. For strength, the tenon and the male parts of other joints must be cut parallel to the grain. Cuts across the grain weaken the timbers. In addition, joints must be cut on dry wood. Any joints fashioned from wood above equilibrium moisture content (see chapter 3) will loosen as the wood dries out.

Some joints were pegged with 5/8-inch-square red elm pegs run through square holes cut through the beam *and* the tenon to effectively *lace* the post and beam together. Usually the hole in the mortised beam is placed about 1/16 inch higher than the hole in the post, so they are slightly misaligned

Left: Curved log beam (*hari*) that spans room in guesthouse interlocks with post in a double mortise and tenon, necessary because this *hari* connects directly to the post rather than to the perimeter beam, which is the more common practise.

Right: The beam in place.

[1] In Japanese construction a perimeter beam and many of the other components are massive, often 5 x 10, 6 x 12, even 7 x 14 or larger. Therefore, in order to avoid giving the reader the impression that these components are the same as in Western timber framing, whose components function somewhat differently, we will frequently refer to them by their Japanese names.

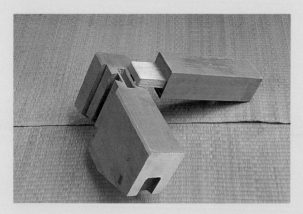

Actual mortise and tenon joint used at underside of a perimeter beam (*keta*). (The rest of the post and *keta* have been cut away.) The *keta* is upside-down with a post tenon resting on it. The joint would be located at the intersection of a hip rafter over two intersecting *ketas*, all supported by a post below.

Joint assembled. Post tenon fits into *keta* mortise. Female dovetail, cut into side of beam, will receive the male dovetail of perpendicular beam. Male beam housing is cut into side of this *keta*, and hip rafter seats are cut into top.

Keta's male dovetail is cut in the shop for installation in the above type of corner assembly at the guesthouse.

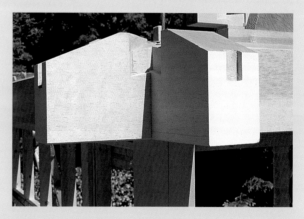

Guesthouse corner joint assembled, hip not yet installed.

Hip being installed.

Hip installed.

when assembled. The peg, called a draw peg, has a beveled end, and as it passes through the tenon, it pushes the tenon up and the beam down, effectively drawing them together in a tighter joint. Multiple tenons can be used in a single joint if the timbers are large enough to require additional strength. In some of East Wind's doors, double mortise and tenons are used to join the door pieces, since increasing the surface area of these joints makes them stronger.

The tenons for structural members can be as short as 4.5 inches; longer ones might pass all the way through a perimeter beam emerging at the top. In cases where great hold-down strength is necessary, they can be wedged from above making withdrawal almost impossible, much the way an ax or a hammer head is attached to a handle by driving wedges into the end as it emerges. This is especially effective if the width of the mortise is expanded at the top of the beam and the wedges are precisely made to "fill" the space in the widened mortise. In windy locations (tops of mountains, on ridges, any place with a great view or where strong winds are likely), wind uplift and lateral wind loading are considerations. The wedged *keta* is essential in these situations, since the eaves of Japanese houses are extensive and present a large surface to wind gusts.

Brackett will sometimes use glue in addition to the traditional means of securing joints, but only in joinery where uplift is a concern. It was used in the guesthouse for finish elements—all the doors and the wide floor panel in the *tokonoma*. "This is about making houses," Brackett explains, "and whatever will do the trick is worth trying. With the kind of adhesives available today, all kinds of possibilities arise. The strength of these glues

Left: Interior view of a finished roof-hip assembly in a home in Marin County, California. When all joints are concealed, the complicated craftsmanship almost appears simple.

Above: In another house, the completed vaulted roof has two valley rafter assemblies, similar to the hip in the left photo.

The back of a *hafu* (barge rafter) showing the pitched female dovetail and the male dovetail on the purlin that will hold the *hafu* in place.

Looking across the length of the ridge and purlin, the above joint can be seen assembled.

added to the traditional pegs and wedges makes the already extremely effective joinery almost indestructible."

Dovetail The dovetail is a fan-shaped joint that usually slides into a pocket cut to fit it exactly. While it can be slid out again, it is intended to pull two pieces of lumber together and hold them there. It, too, is extremely strong and is widely used in Japanese houses. While it isn't the best way to hold a post's foot to the end of a sill, it was perfect for connecting a log to a beam or any two right-angle beams in the guesthouse. Where the *hari* (the huge log beam that spans a room and supports the roof) joins the *keta*, the dovetail is narrower at the bottom and wider at the top, so that upon insertion from above the wedge shape of the joint cinches tightly, yet it is still reasonably easy to assemble. Dovetails were also used at all right-angle connections of purlins, ridges, and sills.

Sometimes a beam cannot be slid into place from above and must be inserted instead into the face of the receiving piece. In such a case a spline dovetail joint is employed. In the guesthouse, this joint connects the short tie beams from the main *keta* of the lean-to roof to a post of the main structure. The end of the tie beam was fitted to the post in a mortise-and-tenon joint. Its tenon was inserted straight into the post, since like all tenons it wouldn't go in unless put in straight. With the tenon secured at the post, the dovetail on the other end of this short beam could not be elevated to slide into the top of the primary *keta* supporting the lean-to roof. As a result, the dovetail end was inserted straight into a cavity cut to receive it, *except* that the narrowest part of the cavity, the neck, was cut so that it was exactly the dimension of the head of the male dovetail. Of course, such a joint would be loose, but here the spline comes to the rescue. Parallelogram-shaped splines are driven into the assembled joint from above to fill the voids left between the male dovetail and the sides of the female joint. They secure the joint almost as tightly as a standard dovetail. A version of this joint is commonly used to secure the *hafu* (barge rafters) to the ends of purlins, ridges and *keta*. (A barge rafter is a wide board at the end of a gable that gives a roof its shape.) A different tapered dovetail, shown above, was used for the barge rafters in the guesthouse.

The blind dovetail or *jigoku ari* (which Brackett jokingly translates as "the dovetail from hell") is cleverly designed and difficult to make. First, a square mortise is cut in the piece of wood that is to receive another at a ninety-degree angle. Then this cavity is widened at its base into a dovetail shape. A square tenon is cut in the male piece of wood so that it won't quite reach the floor of the mortise. Small wedges are inserted into the

tenon's end, so that on insertion into the mortise, the wedges hit the floor of the hole and are driven back into the end of the tenon. This widens the tenon, transforming it into a male dovetail. If done correctly the joint will be tight and the tenon cannot be withdrawn. If done incorrectly either the joint will be loose or the tenon won't go in all the way. In either case, the joint can't be undone for adjusting—and this makes it "the dovetail from hell." It was not used in the guesthouse, but it is commonly called on for built-in desks in other houses.

When the entire house is assembled using hundreds of these two principal joints in so many different forms and locations, *they all work together,* lending the building great resilience in the face of wind loads, earthquakes, and age, since the joints won't rot if kept dry, and they won't corrode or rust like metal fastenings.

Scarf Joints Another class of joinery was also used in the guesthouse, joints that *extend* the length of a component. For example, it is difficult to find pieces of lumber that can run the entire length of the timber frame to serve as perimeter beams or the ridge, but multiple timbers can be

(Clockwise from top)
Female dovetail and housing in *keta* are cut by hand with a saw and chisel following lines drawn in ink.

The same *keta* beam with cuts complete, ready to receive the log beam (*hari*).

The log beam with a male dovetail on the end (not visible) is inserted into the *keta* shown in previous photo.

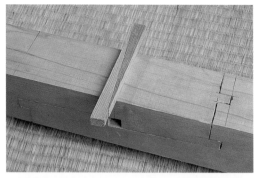

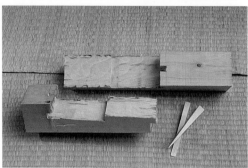

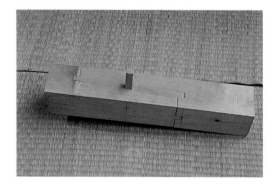

Two opposing wedges will evenly force the members of a swallowtail joint, *kanawa tsugi*, into each other to cinch a scarf joint. Wedges will protrude from sides of assembled joint or they can be cut off flush and finish planed once the joint is made tight.

Swallowtail joint disassembled. It will use the wedge assembly shown above to push it tight.

The swallowtail, assembled.

Above right: A similar version of a swallowtail joint in use to connect two purlins, end to end, over a free span in the guesthouse gallery.

"scarfed"—joined end to end—and made longer. Kiyoshi Seike, in his *The Art of Japanese Joinery*, states that the English term "scarf" derives from the Old Norse word *skarfr*, meaning "obliquely cut beam-end."

There are many versions of these oblique cuts. In the guesthouse, where the *keta* come together over a post, a *daimochi tsugi* was used to make two *keta* one. The *kanawa tsugi*, a very elegant and intriguing joint, sometimes known as a swallowtail, extended the guesthouse's purlins and ridges. This joint is frequently used in a free span, when it isn't possible to position the joint over a post because other pieces are joined there. Occasionally the swallowtail is used to repair a post if the lower portion rots. The damaged part can be replaced with a fresh section of post. It can also be employed to connect a post to a length of granite at its base, so that the wood doesn't sit in soil or water that will cause rot. The granite is sized and cut precisely like the wood and the joint is cut right into it. With a granite foot, a post can even stand in a pond.

The *kama tsugi*, sometimes called a gooseneck, is frequently used where it can be supported from below. It extended the ground sills, *dodai*, in the guesthouse and was supported by the underlying foundation. This joint is usually cut square to the timber, not obliquely. It is relatively easy to make, which is why it is seen so often. It isn't particularly attractive, however, because the mating ends come together with a vertical line, and after a time a slight gap will appear. The head of this joint doesn't pull it together with the same force as other scarf joints. If the mating faces are cut obliquely it is much easier to eliminate the gap so the joint isn't noticeable.

Chiseling or sawing wood to make a joint weakens the timber. Great care has to be taken to avoid cutting away too much wood or the joint's structural integrity will be compromised and it might not be able to carry the expected load. This is particularly important where many components come together in the same place—for example, at the corner of a building where a hip rafter goes over two dovetail-joined perimeter beams as a post tenon enters the bottom of the beam. The photos on page 94 show such a joint in the guesthouse. A considerable amount of wood has been removed. A joint's strength comes from balanced design; as much as possible, each member should be equal in strength. Of course no matter how well a joint is designed and made, it will never be stronger than uncompromised, uncut timber.

Still another scarf joint, one that East Wind calls the best scarf joint of all, was used for the *keta* in the meditation wing of the guesthouse. This spline joint, *shatchi sen*, is a variation on the tenon. With this joint a tenon-like extension (or multiple tenons) of the end of a beam fits tightly into a recess cut in another. Parallelogram-shaped, tapered splines (*shatchi*) are driven into corresponding notches cut along the sides of the tenon and its pocket, forcing the tenon into the female. On occasion, a threaded metal rod is used too. It runs from one beam into the next, penetrating about a foot into each. A pocket is opened in the top of both *keta* to provide access for tightening the nuts and washers threaded onto the rod to pull the two timbers together. It has been East Wind's experience, however, that these bolted joints don't age very well even when dry lumber is used. They seem to have little resilience and in a few years the very tight initial connection opens slightly, while years later the *shatchi sen*-joined timbers are still as tight as the day they were put together.

No matter which kind of joint is used, it must be able to resist tension stress, compression force, and twisting. In the Japanese aesthetic, joinery is usually concealed. If hiding the joinery isn't possible, as indeed it frequently isn't, then certain techniques are used to make it as discreet as possible, with a minimum of visual complexity. Since the buildings themselves are complex, highlighting joinery is distracting and reduces the sense of calm the houses are meant to impart. In most cases the line where one piece joins another is all one should be able to see, offering no hint of the intricacies inside.

Having mentally surveyed the array of joints he was going to use, the carpenter was almost ready to prepare the lumber. But before layout started, he had to make some additional decisions. He had to know:

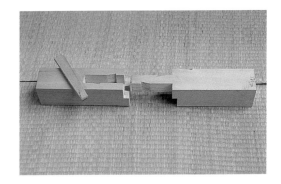

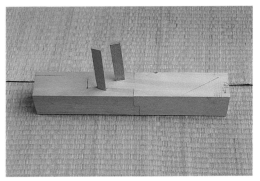

A simple unassembled scarf or spline joint used to join pieces end to end.

The same joint, a *shatchi sen,* assembled.

A scarf joint *(daimochi tsugi)* connects two perimeter beams. Positioning it over a post makes it stronger.

A scarf joint can extend a post or be used to replace rotted wood with new. This unusual scarf joint gives little hint as to how it came together. Its joinery is revealed in the photo on page 103.

▶ The size of the *ken*. This was decided in the initial design process and depended on *which tatami size* was used and the *size of the post*. Even though the guesthouse wasn't going to have tatami, a *ken* dimension was determined to preserve the proportions of space and the building components. There are a variety of *ken* systems throughout Japan, some more complex than others.

▶ The size of the various structural components, that is, the *keta, hari*, rafters, hip rafters, sills, *tsuka* (short posts that support roof structures), door heads, and all the other parts of the house. A larger building will have larger components, especially temples or farmhouses with heavy roofs of slate or tile, or roofs designed to support snow. Delicate teahouses and *sukiya* architecture usually employ the smallest components, while those of fancier houses fall somewhere in the middle.

▶ The dimensions of all the most common joints. Larger components obviously have larger and heavier joinery. The *toryo* decides the length of the dovetails and the width of their heads and necks. The crucial dimensions of the post tenons that connect the post to the groundsills and to the perimeter beams have to be determined. Will the post tenons be pegged in place, wedged in place, not fixed with any mechanism at all, or even glued? The tenons of the short posts may call for another dimension. The carpenter tries to standardize the joints used in a project as much as possible to save time and reduce the possibility of mistakes. He knows that special situations will always crop up where he can either customize a joint or even invent one.

THREE LAYOUT TOOLS

How can the joints be drawn so accurately that they interlock perfectly? How can they be drawn on the timber in precisely the right location? There are hundreds of joinery connections, and keeping them all in mind seems impossible. But this is a building *system*, and three ancient tools—the *kensao*, the story pole, and the *gensun*—are the secret of the Japanese carpenter's success.

The *kensao* is a wonderful measuring stick calibrated anew for each building to lay out horizontal parts and the roof structure. Three drawings in the appendix indicate its use. It locates exactly where the joints are to be made and guarantees absolute uniformity of length, so mistakes in measuring are much less likely. Measuring these dimensions with a tape measure requires multiple checks, and even then mistakes are made if the tape is misread or it slips out of position on the wood.

The *toryo* made the *kensao* for the guesthouse from a straight, dry and defect-free piece of wood about $1\,^1/_2$ inches wide by $1\,^1/_2$ inches thick and about 3 *ken* (about 19 feet) long. Its use is worth describing in some detail.

The drawing of the *kensao* on Appendix page 196 is "unwrapped" to show all four faces. It presents a foreshortening of the entire *kensao*, showing a half-*ken*, one *ken*, one and a half *ken*, and two *ken* centerlines with appropriate joint-component locations. These centerlines are the points from which all dimensions are laid out. Also shown is a mark indicating the *theoretical* inside surface of the female piece. It is "theoretical" because even though every effort is made to keep the timbers uniform, exceptions always arise, either because a piece needs to be larger for structural reasons or because it "wouldn't make planing" and is "scant" (less than the required dimension). This could be the result of milling errors, or a warp could develop in the lumber as it dries, forcing the carpenter straightening it to remove more than he wants from the ends or the middle. In most houses, such unexpected variations appear.

If the lumber used to make any of the components isn't uniform, then the layout of the building can become particularly difficult and time consuming. All the exceptions made in dimensioning the joinery for, let us say, hundreds of female dovetails would have to be remembered when laying out the male components. However, unless the female is very much smaller than expected, these discrepancies will *automatically* be accounted for with the *kensao*. Even if the female timber is smaller (or larger) than intended, the location of the neck of the male dovetail that plunges into it will not change, as it will be a fixed distance off the centerline that runs the length of the female timber. This means that all male timbers of the same type will be exactly the same, and all dimensional discrepancies will be accounted for only in the depth of the recession of the female timber. Woodworkers take careful note. *Because of these variations, Japanese layout is always made measuring from centerline to centerline of all structural elements, almost never surface to surface.* This centerline running the length of the female timber will always be the same, no matter how large the timber, and it isn't subject to the vagaries of milling, warping, or shrinkage.

The top face of the *kensao* in the illustration is devoted to the *keta* and the purlins, which run the length of the building, and has almost all the

Measurements

So far, we have quoted dimensions in feet and inches, but many skilled Japanese carpenters use neither the American system nor the international metric system of measure. Theirs is a third system, the traditional *shaku*, which Brackett finds more practical both for mathematical calculations and for use in the shop and on site.

It is useful to think of the *shaku* as a one-foot length. It is precisely 11.930406 inches long or about $^1/_{16}$ inch short of a foot. The *shaku* is divided into ten divisions, each called a *sun*. The *sun* is divided into ten parts called *bu*. The *bu* is again divided into ten sections called *rin*. And believe it or not, the *rin* is again divided into 10 *mo*, although *mo* are really too small to distinguish with the naked eye. Dimensions are expressed in decimals, and in East Wind's usage, 1 *shaku* is expressed as 1.000 *shaku*, and a *sun* is 0.100.

Instead of chalk, a string reeled through India ink in this container snaps straight lines. A bamboo pen is used with a square to make very fine cut lines, finer than any pen and perfectly indelible. The layout lines are planed off in the final finishing process.

The conversion factors are as follows:
1 *shaku* = 11.930406 inches
1 *shaku* = 0.9942005 feet
1 foot = 1.0058333 *shaku*
1 *sun* = 1.193 inches = about 1 $^1/_4$ inches
1 *bu* = 0.193 inches = about an $^1/_8$ inch

The advantages of using the *shaku* system, according to Brackett, is that it combines the human scale of the British system with a base-10 system, thereby making it unnecessary to calculate in clumsy base-12 inches or in fractions, which is time-consuming. More important, fractions often require rounding measurements up and down slightly, introducing inaccuracies. If a small inaccuracy is repeated several times, for example, between parts of a grating, the cumulative error becomes very significant. A calculator with many decimal places can reduce the cumulative error to an imperceptible level. Brackett rules out metric measurements because he finds a millimeter too large for accurate work and smaller metric dimensions too small to read easily or to calibrate on a measuring instrument like a square. A measuring tool with tenths of millimeters would be unreadable and therefore unuseable.

At the end of the nineteenth century, the Japanese government chose to adopt the metric measuring system to simplify international trading and to become part of the rest of the world. The *shaku* measure was not only abandoned, it became illegal. The craftsmen of Japan, like most craftsmen everywhere being wed to their way of doing things, ignored the legislation and turned to buying their measuring tools calibrated in *bu*, *sun*, and *shaku* under the counter. When Brackett was in Japan in the 1970s, a lively underground industry thrived to supply these illegal tools for carpenters and other traditional craftsmen who didn't want to relinquish the more convenient traditional system. He vividly remembers the consternation of one of his fellow carpenters whose sister was investigated by the authorities for manufacturing *shaku*-calibrated yardsticks (three *shaku* measures). Recently the government relented, and now *bu-sun-shaku* tools can be purchased legally. In fact, the Japanese Institute of Standards (JIS, which is similar to the National Bureau of Standards in the U.S.) now sanctions and has standardized this traditional ancient measure.

Brackett's shop uses the *shaku* because it is close to the foot, which he, his staff, and his clients are accustomed to using. Although Japanese hand and power tools along with woodworking machines are sold calibrated with the metric system, it just happens that three millimeters is very close to one *bu*. Dividing millimeters by three lets Japanese carpenters work in terms of the *shaku* system (for example, 9 mm divided by 3 = 3 *bu*), so most tooling comes in 3, 6, 9 12, 15, 18, 21 mm sizes.

information needed to lay out these pieces accurately. The next face is devoted to the *hari* and some of the other transverse timbers, with all their layout measurements. It also indicates the locations of *tsuka*, the short posts supporting the ridge and purlins, which are connected to transverse beams (whether *hari* or *keta*) running the width of the structure. The third face is intended for laying out the *dodai*, while the bottom face is simply a *shaku* measuring scale of whole *shaku* increments, frequently marked with dimensions of tatami or multiples of tatami. The basic *ken* module is shown plainly on all four faces as the Centerline, CL. The *ken* for a particular structure never varies once it has been determined, whether it is used to position posts or determine the length of the *keta*, *hari*, or *dodai*.

The face of the *kensao* shown in the drawing Kensao Keta Yuki on Appendix page 195 was used to lay out the *keta*, the purlins, and ridges, as well as to locate the centers of the *hari*, which are supported by the *keta* and whose joints come at intervals shown on the *kensao*. The drawing shows the *keta yuki* (*keta* direction) axis of the building, which usually runs the length of the building. At the top are elevational drawings showing the roof structure (*keta* and purlins) from the side. Below them is a simplified *kensao* with "*keta* face of *kensao*" written on it. Below that is a sample *keta* assembly in plan view, looking down on it.

The first step in laying out the guesthouse was marking the centerlines along the length of the lumber. They can be set by snapping a straight ink line down the middle of the timber, or, if the timbers are uniform, by running a marking gauge down their length that leaves a cut exactly in the middle. This is usually done on surfaces that won't be visible in the finished structure—the tops of beams, bottoms of pieces below eye level, or components that will be obscured by other building elements such as a wall.

It should be remembered that any location in any given plane in the building can be determined by the intersection of two centerlines. In a *keta*, for example, one of these centerlines will run the *keta*'s length, usually marked along the top, and the other would be at a right angle to it, where another timber would be attached to it.

The *kensao* was used to mark the points on the female timber where its centerline crosses the centerline of the male piece, and they were laid out using the square, bamboo pen, and a marking gauge. The *kensao* was also used to mark all the appropriate details of the male joint, including where the tenon or the dovetail starts and ends—where the neck (the narrow part) of the dovetail is and where the head (the widest part) of the dovetail is, or in other words, the length of the standard dovetail.

A view of the interior of the trick joint shown on page 100. Whalers carved scrimshaw; Japanese carpenters have fun with wood in their spare time.

The female joint will almost always have not only a female dovetail or a mortise cut into the timber to receive the male dovetail or the tenon but also a "housing." A housing is a shallow recess or pocket, usually cut into the side of a beam containing the female portion of the dovetail. This shallow cut, usually between a half-inch to one inch deep, is shaped to exactly fit the end of the male timber. When the joint is assembled, this housing holds the end of the beam and prevents it from warping or twisting. The female dovetail cut or the mortise is made deeper into the beam, deeper even than the housing. The dovetail or mortise and tenon pull the two pieces together and hold them tightly; the housing serves to prevent twisting and to make the joint appear seamlessly tight. The *kensao* does *not* set the depth of the housing, but it determines the length of the timber with male joints at its end(s) and the proportions of its dovetail. Every male timber in a series is laid out using the *kensao* so they will all be precisely the same length. The depth of the housing is *always set from the centerline running the length of the timber that contains the female joint* Idiosyncrasies in the thickness of the female timber will then be accounted for *only in the varying depth of this housing, not in the length or proportions of the male timber or its dovetail.* (See the lower section of the drawing entitled Kensao Keta Yuki.)

The drawing on page 197 entitled Kensao Hari Yuki shows the use of the *kensao* for laying out a log beam and locating the positions of the short posts that support the purlins and ridges. Though it isn't shown in the drawing, this face of the *kensao* can also indicate the centerlines for positioning pegged hanging posts on the transverse timbers to support door and window heads (*kamoi*). Just as with the *keta*, the *hari* also fit into a housing, but these *hari* are usually faceted on their bottom surfaces to ensure good bearing surfaces and to speed the work. Transferring facets to a beam is much easier than trying to shape a housing to the natural contours of an eccentric and natural round log. Sometimes shaping is done, but only in very fancy work. The housing for the *hari* is usually a bit deeper than one used for *keta*, and the dovetail is usually a wedge-shaped dovetail, narrower at the bottom than at the top. The top third or so of the *hari* frequently overlaps the top of the supporting *keta*. These *hari* can sometimes carry great roof loads. Just as with the *keta kensao*, the *hari kensao* will automatically account for discrepancies in the dimension of the *keta* into which the *hari* is joined.

The *kensao* is placed on the piece to be marked and its measurements transferred to the wood with the carbon-black ink. In making the mark-

The modern blueprint works in tandem with a *kensao*, a measuring stick indicating distance between the centerlines of all components. An ancient concept, it ensures that all joints are cut in the right place.

ings, the *toryo* constantly tries to highlight interesting characteristics. He slides the *kensao* back and forth along the length of the piece, positioning the stick where the cuts will reveal the wood's best features, while making sure that knots and other defects will be cut away as the piece is trimmed for length or at least obscured inside a joint.

The benefits of the *kensao* are many:

1. The carpenter doesn't have to remember the exact dimensions of each joint and correlate them to other pieces, some of which may not even be milled or are under another pile of lumber. The *kensao* remembers them. It is so easy to become muddled and inadvertently assign the wrong joint to a location, i.e., make a dovetail for a *keta* that should be used for the purlin.

2. Calculating differing irregularities in lumber mathematically takes a lot more time and mistakes are much more likely to occur. The *kensao* automatically accounts for them.

3. A tape measure is awkward since it has a tendency to slip off the lumber, bend, or wobble around. Accurately measuring from the hook end of a tape measure is difficult, with the result that one has to "kill a foot"—measure from the one-foot mark rather than from the end of the tape. Mistakes happen when the carpenter forgets he killed a foot and his measurement is a foot too long. The *kensao* will be accurate at each of its ends, and it will stay flat on the lumber so marking both ends is accurate and easy.

4. The *kensao* shows the actual joinery, while the tape doesn't.

5. Measuring is physical with the stick, not theoretical as with a numerically calibrated measuring device. Theory and reality are more easily confused using numbers rather than the actual space shown on the *kensao*.

6. With the stick, transposing dimensions and dividing them into increments is done *before* the lumber calls for it, not in the rush of working. It need only be done once, with extreme care.

7. The *kensao* is rigid, making it superior in laying out a curving log because it won't sag from a straight line like a tape.

8. The *kensao* can also be taken to the site and be used to check the accuracy of the foundation, since it physically represents the building being prepared in the shop hundreds of miles away.

9. Even if minor mistakes are made, at least they'll be consistent with a *kensao*, which probably wouldn't be the case with a tape measure, since the marks on the *kensao* measure everything using a set series of marks.

In earlier times, when the house was completed, the *kensao* was left behind and stored in the open space above the ceiling so a future carpenter had a record of its layout and could use it in making any additions or repairs. Because all the rooms were modular rectangles or squares based upon the *ken* particular to the house, the house could be readily expanded as the family grew in size or its fortunes improved, without having to redesign. East Wind regularly leaves the unique tool behind; the *kensao* for the guesthouse is tucked above a ceiling. For three centuries most houses in Japan were built according to this system.

Another helpful layout tool is the story pole (*hashira no kensao* or post *kensao*), a pole that is a little longer than the tallest post in the house. It showed all the critical heights of the guesthouse components that related to the posts and walls, and was used to indicate where the posts should be cut to receive them. These included the tie beams and transverse beams, ceiling moldings, door and window heads and sills, finish flooring, floor supports (*kamachi*), and any other member tied to the post. It also showed the length of the tenons at the top and bottom of post. And, like the *kensao*, it too was positioned on the best spot on the lumber where defects could be minimized or hidden.

Brackett with full-scale layout of the roof structure of the guesthouse. Called a *gensun* and drawn in ink on plywood, the *gensun* is used most often in construction of ceremonial architecture where many curves have to be cut exactly.

A third device, the *gensun*, aided with the preparation of the roof structure and is used if a roof is particularly curved or has other complexities to be worked out. A full-scale layout of the roof or a portion of it was drawn on $1/8$-inch plywood. This process (nearly identical to the shipbuilding technique called "lofting") is especially important in complex ceremonial buildings, and requires a great deal of floor space if the entire roof has to be drawn full scale. (Usually only the part that curves needs to be drawn.) Each of the different curves is drawn on the *gensun*, and then the lines are transferred to boards or other pieces of plywood to make templates. The templates (*kata ita* or "form boards") become the patterns for cutting out the difficult curved components. Since the guesthouse roof was thick and its curves more severe than East Wind's usual roofs, its facia and eaves detail members couldn't bend at the curved hips as they would with a thinner roof. The curves of the eave structural components had to be accurately determined and cut in the shop before going to site, and to do that a *gensun* was required.

MATCHLESS TOOLS

When all the joints were marked, the lumber was turned over to a crew of about five men to carefully reduce the pieces to their proper dimensions following the layout lines. At this stage, as many as fifteen carpenters can work together at East Wind. The team's work proceeded in strict accordance with a critical path schedule to ensure that components and joints were prepared in the most efficient sequence possible.

Although the Japanese house is always pre-cut in the shop, it is not pre- assembled; that would be too time-consuming and too costly. What's more, since these joints are very tight, disassembling them is apt to permanently damage the pieces. As a result, the carpenters have to be skilled, their work must be accurate, and not until the house is assembled will they know how well they did.

Even skillful craftsmen can execute precise joinery only with the best tools. Those needed for making handmade joints are saws, mortising chisels, finish chisels, slicks (long-handled push chisels) hammers, and hand planes.

Like the renowned samurai sword, Japanese woodworking tools are masterpieces in laminated steel. The techniques involved in laminating originated in ancient China and were copied by the Syrians, who produced the famous Damascus steel. The Japanese also took up this new technology and refined it even further, as they have with so many of the world's ideas and technologies. By the seventh century, just one hundred years after steel's first appearance in Japan, the finest steel found in China came from Japan. Laminated steel is created by welding together a very hard and brittle layer of edge steel (*hagane*) with a softer, more malleable, shock-absorbing steel (*jigane*) to form a single blade that combines the best qualities of both types and which is almost magically sharp and tough. As steel becomes harder, it also becomes more brittle and more likely to shatter on impact. Soft steel, on the other hand, is malleable and able to absorb great shock, but it won't take or keep a keen edge. Welding the two together results in a blade that withstands shock, as when a chisel is hammered into a hard knot on a piece of wood. It also has a very sharp edge that stays sharp even after frequent use.

These tools are truly "razor sharp"—one really can shave with them. "We were in Tokyo building a main gate, six stories high, for Kanda Shrine," recalls Brackett with a smile, "at the end of the day, we would all troop down to the very beautiful public bath to get cleaned up. We were covered with the red dye used to stain the building, and as we all sat together soaping up, a great cloud of pink soapsuds would go scudding across the floor. The first time I went, I realized I had left my razor in Kyoto, so for several weeks I shaved with the blade of my hand plane."

The ultimate example of laminated steel is the samurai sword, which has as many as twenty thousand layers of steel laminated together. In the mid-nineteenth century, the new imperial government banned the wearing of swords, and it appeared that the ancient lineages of sword smiths would end. Fortunately, many of these sword smiths turned to carpentry tools and produced some of the finest woodworking tools ever made, as their descendants still do today. Some hold that the quality of steel in the best carpentry tools is better today than it was three hundred years ago, though perhaps not as good as during the second half of the nineteenth century, when former sword smiths were making them. Still, there are a few outstanding exceptions today. Of the few younger tool makers still genuinely committed to the craft, one in particular, Funahiro, employs modern chemistry and metallurgical techniques along with the traditional skills he learned as an apprentice to make blades that rival the best ever made.

Today's tools are still expensive. A fine plane can easily cost a thousand dollars, and if, like the one pictured on this page, it was made by a famous craftsman, it can be many times that. The plane in the photo was made by

A plane blade showing the steel laminations that make Japanese tools so remarkably sharp.

Sharpening a plane blade

Japanese chisels are all handmade and sharp as razors.
Knives in right foreground are for sculpting scrollwork.

Three common hammers. At left is a sculptor's heavy hammer, custom-made to the carpenter's specifications, used for making short and frequent strikes. The middle one is for driving nails or "killing wood." Its rounded face slightly crushes male components, making them a bit smaller, before they are slid into a tight joint. On the right is a general use hammer whose tapered end is used to adjust a plane blade.

Five different kinds of saws: (l. to r.) a rip saw (over 100 years old) for large tenons, a general use combination crosscut/rip saw, another rip saw for cutting delicate tenons, a back saw for very fine crosscuts, and an *azebiki* to make a cut starting in the middle of a board. Saws at right are protectively sheathed.

Plane at left is for chamfering, next two for general planing. Fourth is a specialized jointing plane used to make a surface perfectly flat or straight. Also pictured are an adze and a broad ax.

Chiozuru Tadahide, one of the most famous plane makers in Japan. Most of the tools shown in the photographs in this book were handmade in the ancient tradition, and a few of them are over a hundred years old. Some of these tools were given to Brackett by Kobori Roshi, who received them from a widow of a craftsman who makes the beautiful paulownia boxes in which scrolls are kept. Many others were given to him by his teachers and by his fellow carpenters in Japan.

Tool-making apprenticeship in Japan lasts about fifteen years, and many techniques used by individual toolmakers are secret. Additives such as a paste of soil are put around the blade in the firing process to improve its quality, or special straw is used in the firing. These secrets have been handed down without interruption, each generation refining and adding to the technique. At the final tempering the doors of the workshop are closed, the windows shut, and the work takes place in the dark to allow the toolmaker to see the glow of the red-hot steel and let its color indicate when it is the right temperature to plunge it into water for its final tempering.

At the moment, Japan retains an inconceivably vast body of knowledge and a few people who are almost magically skilled at producing these unrivaled tools. However, implements of this quality are becoming rare, since today's youth aren't interested in the commitment and time necessary to learn how to make them, particularly with so many other less demanding career options available. By the time Japan realizes what has slipped away, the teachers will be gone and the skills will be lost forever.

There are, of course, many kinds of steel made around the world today. There is steel to cut steel, steel to cut wood or meat, steel to make die cuts, rust-resistant steel, and the list goes on and on. Most modern steel manufacturers in the West who make tools for cutting wood use various alloys and tempering processes in the attempt to combine hardness and toughness in a single unforged piece, but the results leave much to be desired. Generally the edge of such steel cannot compare in keenness to that of laminated steel, and if it does, it dulls quickly. William H. Coaldrake, whose book *The Way of the Carpenter* is devoted to Japanese tools, cites a recent comparison of the performance of Japanese- and Western-made chisels that demonstrates that the hand-forged Japanese chisel blades held their cutting edge up to six times longer than those mass-produced by the Western drop-forged method.

Generally, Japanese tools are used with a pulling motion rather than the pushing motion that is characteristic of their Western counterparts: the Japanese saw cuts on the pull stroke; the plane is pulled, not pushed.

Whetstones make tools perfectly sharp. Many of these rare stones came from Aoyama in Takao north of Kyoto, source of the finest finish stones (*awaseido*) in Japan. The white stone in the middle is a remarkably good man-made stone that has only recently become available.

Brackett feels there is a lot more control in pulling a tool rather than pushing it, since pulling allows the entire body to control the motion. Pulling the Japanese plane, which has the blade in the back third of the block rather than up in the front, creates a different geometry, making the plane more effective at making a perfectly flat cut, so that a continuous, uninterrupted surface can be finished or an edge can be mated to another with no apparent joint. The superiority of Japanese tools is gradually gaining recognition, and Japanese saws, inklines, and marking gauges are appearing on American building supply shelves and in tool catalogs.

SHARPENING STONES

There isn't much point in having superior blades and chisels without a whetstone capable of maintaining the quality of the steel. The finest traditional finish stones come from Aoyama Mountain near Kyoto. Without question, these natural stones, called *honyama awase* when they come from Aoyama Mountain, are considered the best, and they are very beautiful, each one unique. Most have been formed under the ocean's bed of volcanic dust and compressed for millions of years. Until recently carpenters had to resign themselves to spending a fortune for large stones without natural defects.

But just as Funahiro is using new technologies in combination with the old to make superb blades, so too are new stones being developed that aren't from a mountain at all, but which employ newly developed ceramic technologies to produce stones that rival natural ones, and in some cases surpass them. The ceramic Shapton stone is an economical substitute for the *honyama awase* stone. It stays flat a very long time, sharpens quickly, and produces a superbly polished edge. Diamond technology has also come a long way, so that diamond "stones," while of little use for producing the finish edge, are extremely useful for the initial stages of sharpening. They are excellent for shaping the blade, removing chips, and flattening the backs of blades. One of the problems in sharpening a plane is putting the proper curve—a "rocker"—in the blade. This curve is usually only a few thousandths of an inch off a straight line, and it takes years to develop a sense of how to do it. With a diamond stone, however, a perfectly straight line can be made across the edge of a plane blade, and then that line can be adjusted fairly easily to arrive at the right rocker, which is more curved for a rough plane blade than for a finish plane

In another surprising development, stores such as Hida Tool in Berkeley, California, carry aluminum oxide powder to be placed on a flat piece of wood in tiny quantities, so that the *wood becomes the stone* for the final finish. The resulting steel shines like a mirror and is so sharp it can literally split hairs

Brackett remembers when, as an apprentice, he visited two or three sharpening stone specialty shops in Kyoto that sold only hand-sharpening stones. Once the proprietors got to know him, they would sell him a stone with the expectation that he would try it for a couple of weeks and return with his reaction. If it wasn't exactly what he was looking for, they gave him another to try. Some stones were better for blades used for *hinoki*, and some were better for blades for *sugi*. It took about five or six attempts before he found what he wanted. He used his prize stones until 1985 when a visitor, who came to one of the construction sites to get some sharpening advice, came back at night and stole his most valued stones and some other tools as well. Sadly, the thief doesn't even know the value of what he took.

Much of the ability to care for and use these tools hinges on developing an eye trained to identify whether a blade is really sharp, to see the curve of the plane-blade edge and the set of a hand-plane blade. A skilled carpenter

Hollow chisel mortising bit cuts square holes to receive 5/8-inch-square pegs of red elm, an ideal wood for pegs since it is hard yet pliable. This machine saves enormous amounts of time.

can re-sharpen an edge in five minutes, while a new apprentice can spend the entire day on a single blade and still not get it right. For every eight hours of work with a particular tool, a skilled carpenter spends perhaps as little as thirty minutes keeping it perfectly sharp, which may involve re-honing it every thirty to sixty minutes if it is in constant use.

Brackett uses both fine Japanese hand tools and power tools in his workshop. He says that for simple repeat joinery a machine can produce work that may even be better than hand cut. In such cases, as long as quality isn't compromised, machinery is gratefully used. This also pleases his clients, who generally prefer not to pay for needless labor. Since there are so many joints, all the layout tools, marking gauges, and power tools can be set and used over and over again without taking the time to customize each connection. A skilled craftsman using the finest hand tools, however, can complete very fine work with amazing speed. "Most observers are astounded at the apparent ease and speed with which these men do this fine work," comments Brackett.

Though there is always a temptation to design a house in a way that maximizes the ease of construction with the exclusive use of machinery, Brackett believes that this isn't a good idea. Machinery has its place, certainly, but he urges that such a temptation be resisted if machined joinery isn't perfectly suited for its intended use. Machined joinery reduces the fluency of the carpenter to employ all his tricks, all his approaches to design; perhaps more critical to the client, it forces the design to remain within the limits of what a machine can do. "Essentially it should be the carpenter's option to use machines; the machine shouldn't dictate the design," says Brackett.

In talking about the interrelationships of Japanese trades, Brackett invents a term: "old-growth culture." He says, "In old-growth ecosystems, each ecological niche is filled with creatures that exploit every imaginable kind of symbiosis, relationship, and alliance, making the entire system amazingly complex and stable. This is how it is in the world of carpentry and woodworking in Japan. Great carpentry demands great tools, a great sharpening stone, great plastering, great copper roof work, great fittings and metal work, and so forth. The old-growth culture involved in building is only a small component of a much larger old-growth culture, Japan itself, which today is just as threatened as the forests of the world."

After being away from Japan for many years, Brackett returned to visit his mentor, Hide Tadayuki, and went with him to buy tools for his apprentices back in California: "He took me to a wholesaler who had the most incredible collection of tools I had ever seen. At one point in our meeting I had to go out to the car to get something and in my absence, Hide-san asked if we might see the Tetsunosuke saws. When I came back in, these saws—the finest made—were out on the counter. Tools as rare as these are usually not displayed and are offered for sale only to those who the seller believes measure up to them and can appreciate their fineness. My teacher took me aside and told me that the shopkeeper had agreed to sell me one.

"I remember panicking, thinking there was no way I could afford such a saw. Yet not to buy it would be an insult. I acted thrilled, even though I was very concerned, and was preparing to spend all the money I had. I expressed my deep gratitude and with a shudder asked the price. The answer was twenty-five thousand yen, about one hundred dollars at the time. I was amazed, since I knew that such a saw was worth at least two thousand dollars then, and probably many times that now. The shop owner remarked in an offhand way that this was what the price tag said. When I expressed surprise, he mentioned that it was an old tag—in fact twenty or more years old, adding that 'changing the cost, once I've priced it, is bad form, and I don't do that here.'"

As is true of so many aspects and objects of everyday life in Japan, woodworking tools are surrounded with religious rituals. Coaldrake emphasizes this point: "Carpentry was as worthy of devotion as any religious faith and never lacked suitable aspirants to its life of discipline and devotion."[2] George Nakashima, another devotee of Japanese craftsmanship, describes one such aspirant in his classic *Soul of a Tree*, retelling a favorite story in Japan about a young man from the country who went to the city and apprenticed himself to a woodworker: "He was convinced that

[2] William H. Coaldrake, *The Way of the Carpenter* (New York: Weatherhill, Inc., 1990), p. 7

this was to be his life's work, and his parents agreed. A simple fellow, he had great determination and capacity in his craft. Back in his village his parents awaited word of his progress. First a year, then another, and finally a third passed, but still no word. The city was not so far, they thought. Why can't he at least visit us? Then, after five years, an envelope arrived. Hastily opening it, they found no letter; all it contained was a long wood shaving, ten feet along, neatly folded and perfect in every way, not a skip anywhere. The simplest of statements, it told it all, like broad simple ink strokes in fine calligraphy. The father, immediately understanding, exclaimed: 'Ah, my son has made it.'"[3]

The story does not exaggerate the intensity of this introductory training. Nor is it apocryphal. When Len Brackett accepted the opportunity to apprentice, he worked under three great temple builders: Hide Tadayuki, Mitsuji Yoshihisa, and Hosomi Tadaki. At the start he was told he was going to be given an opportunity rarely offered to others of his generation. He could straighten, square, and bring to uniform dimension most of the finish elements of the temple under construction *with a hand plane.* This meant that he would spend most of the first two years of his apprenticeship hand planing boards and timbers twelve hours a day, seven days a week, with one day off every two weeks to study and care for his tools. The task was normally accomplished with a jointer and a thickness planer, but these machines were located at the company's shop in Kyoto, far from the remote location of the Shobo-an Temple. In retrospect, Brackett realizes that his teachers took their charge to teach him very seriously, so much so that they were willing to risk a large quantity of valuable lumber by placing it in his hands, even paying him to occasionally ruin it. This was a great gift, occasioned not so much by lack of machinery as by their desire that he learn the old way.

But as Brackett recalls his early experience at hand planing, "There is no more intimate way to learn about wood." He says he learned more than he imagined possible, not only about planing but also about the qualities of various woods. A hand plane, he explains, teaches in a physical and unforgettable way. Feeling the wood through the plane uncovers its true character, which mere looking doesn't. This is why Japanese carpenters talk about wood emotionally, using terms like "stubborn," "cantankerous," "sweet," and "forgiving"—as if the wood were alive, which indeed it is.

In a fitting continuation of this tradition, two of Brackett's apprentices, Dylan "Cedar" Hennings and Eliot Wread, took top honors in 2002 and 2001 in the hand-planing competition of the Kezuro Kai of North America. One

[3] George Nakashima, *The Soul of a Tree* (Tokyo: Kodansha International, 1981), p. 113.

winning shaving was twelve feet long and about two inches wide—and only 0.0012 inches thick. A good strong puff of air from a person's lips can send it floating across the room. Resembling smoke more than wood, it is nearly transparent, with only its long fibers visible. Skilled hand planing leaves behind an unbelievably smooth surface, smoother than can be produced with any sandpaper. The hand-planed surface shines like glass and feels like it as well. Under a microscope, its surface is so smooth that in comparison a sanded finish appears to have been dragged down a gravel road.

As noted earlier, the planed finish is the final finish in traditional Japanese woodworking; rarely is wood sealed, oiled, or painted. When the guesthouse components were hand planed, they were also chamfered or beveled to remove all the sharp corners, another detail of quality carpentry. Even the degree of angle of the bevel is considered. Nothing looks rough or unfinished, no matter how informal the nature of the building. Sometimes this softening is very apparent; sometimes it is extremely subtle, but edges are never left sharp.

Obviously the builder must be highly skilled with the square, the pen, and the inkline. Being adept with them is a rare facility and one that makes a Japanese carpenter more than just a woodworker. Carpenters say it takes years and years to understand the full complexity of their use, since they call for multiple skills. The Japanese carpenter must also be a master of design as well as of woodworking. He must know solid geometry and be able to think in three-dimensional terms. He must know how to lay out the building so that, for example, the curves on the roof running down the hip and swooping down the primary rafters match up with the lift of the eaves and meet at the same place. He also is the only one who decides the shape of the gable and where each type of chamfer is appropriate. He must oversee the felling of timber, direct its milling, and know what size, species, grain pattern, and orientation are appropriate in the building. Essentially he decides all the detailing of the building. But first he has to know how to use a plane. He begins learning layout only after he knows how to use his tools.

As each component was prepared in the shop for the guesthouse, it was protectively wrapped in clear plastic pallet wrap or paper to keep it free of dirt, dust, and fingerprints. There are several advantages to pallet wrap. If it's used to spiral wrap a post from the bottom, it will shed rainwater as long as it isn't perforated. It also adheres to itself like kitchen plastic wrap so lumber stacked in a moving container isn't likely to slide around. In addition, the underlying wood is visible, which can be helpful for taking dimensions or for reading location coding. On the other hand, it is easily torn, and allows sunlight to burn the wood. If water gets in, it can't get out, so there is a risk of mildew. Brackett still prefers it, but some of his carpenters like the traditional paper. The main advantage of paper is that if it gets wet, it at least will dry out, as will the lumber beneath. At the site, the end of the paper gets torn away to show the coordinates.

The wrapped components were placed in an airtight and insulated container for transportation to the site. The container is insulated to keep them from drying out in the sun's heat and from being damaged by condensation at night until they are installed. They stayed wrapped during the assembly process to protect them from damage from evening dew before the roof went up and from dirty hands and muddy work shoes during the building process

A tool trailer, providing an electrical and compressed air system, was also brought to the site. It held everyone's tools, as well as a jointer, planer, table saw on wheels, and a duplicate set of the workshop's power hand tools. Communications equipment—fax, phones, and computer terminals—plus weather stripping, fasteners, and specialized Japanese hardware were also kept in the trailer. At this point, all systems were "go" and the building was ready to be assembled like a giant 3-D jigsaw puzzle.

While most people who are interested in Japanese architecture are intrigued by the joinery involved, which is indeed extraordinary, this book hopes to show that joinery is only part of this rich architectural tradition.

The veranda (*engawa*) of this small building, another
guesthouse, is supported by stones. Hidden behind the
veranda, a stem wall supports the rest of the structure.

GROUNDWORK AND FRAMEWORK

CHOOSING SUBCONTRACTORS

With the shop work completed, the next step involved selecting subcontractors and planning the order of everyone's work on site.

A considerable amount of time was spent determining the best people in California's Bay Area to provide the various systems needed, such as electrical, plumbing, heating, and security. The specialists didn't have to understand Japanese architecture; they simply had to be adaptable, quick on their feet, and very careful not to damage already completed work. The electrician and the plumber had to know, for example, where to drill a hole—and be trusted to ask if they didn't. Companies who had already worked with East Wind were given first consideration, as less time had to be spent briefing them on how things should be done for this exceptional kind of construction.

Subcontracting estimates were studied and judged for completeness. Was the lowest cost real, or were there forgotten—or worse, intentionally omitted—costs, which would have to be paid later by the client or East Wind? Was the estimate unreasonably high? Or was it naïvely low, which would indicate an inexperienced contractor? All this had to be balanced, of course, with whether good work could be done on schedule. Poor work that has to be redone or work that is late wastes huge amounts of money, since succeeding tasks have to wait, and the entire job can no longer be accomplished in an orderly, predictable fashion.

East Wind advises clients that they may either hire a general contractor to coordinate all the subcontractors in conjunction with their woodworking and plastering specialists, or they can hire East Wind to be the contractor and oversee all stages of the construction. The Pawlowskis decided to have East Wind see the project through to completion. In areas where East Wind doesn't know local building officials or the contractors, or where distance makes frequent visits to the site impossible, clients are advised to let someone else oversee the construction. The company's scope of work is then restricted to those tasks that are specific to Japanese design, woodworking, and materials. This doesn't mean, however, that East Wind's involvement with the contractor is limited to scheduling. The company will still be responsible for helping the contractor understand what's going to be required, and a staff member is assigned to track the contractor's work as it proceeds, a task that is calculated into the estimate.

East Wind directed the subcontractors working on the guesthouse and helped them deal with the unpredictable elements—those surprises that occur no matter how carefully the plans are prepared. The art gallery's computerized lighting system, for example, required larger transformers than expected, and more of them. Finding a place to put them was a problem, since they produced more heat than expected, and that, too, had to be dealt with (see chapter 6).

Brackett strongly advises clients not to act as their own general contractors unless the project is very small and limited in scope, or unless they have extensive contracting experience and are willing to devote a considerable amount of time to doing the job properly. How to get the job done, whom to hire, what equipment is needed and available, how to deal with a difficult inspector, how to present the project to the planning department, what kind of materials to get, where to find them—all these aspects of a construction job require experience and full-time involvement. It is definitely not a matter of flipping through the Yellow Pages and making a few phone calls. A lot of time and money are usually wasted when the owner becomes the contractor. The owner's time is already required for all the decisions that only he can make, such as choosing electrical, plumbing, and lighting fixtures, deciding plaster color, and so forth, so he is very much involved anyway. Inexperienced owner-contractors frequently create morale problems among the subcontractors by scheduling tasks improperly, making it impossible for the subcontractors to do their work. Orchestrating a conventional house is difficult and time-consuming enough. For an inexperienced person to try to do this with a Japanese house is presumption in the extreme.

Just as the work in the shop progressed in a strict order, the on-site construction was set up to follow a precise succession of steps, which were entered into a computer project management program. The program, Microsoft Project, converted linked tasks—and those of all the subcontractors—into a bar graph with a timeline, showing which task needed to be done before another could be started, the duration of each task, and number of men needed. The program also made possible an accurate labor-cost analysis. (It doesn't, of course, suggest costs of materials, travel, and the million other attendant expenses like nails, shop supplies, food and lodging, office expense, profit, and so forth.) This schedule, called a critical path, is to the process of construction what drawings are to its design.

Pawlowski says, "I found it absolutely fascinating that East Wind used project-scheduling software and, more important, the AutoCAD design tool, to make what is essentially a traditional Japanese structure whose design roots go back a thousand years. As a computer professional myself, I found the juxtaposition of the modern and the traditional exciting. Think about it: I had carpenters in my backyard hand planing wood, using traditional Japanese saws, hand cutting a house that was drawn using the world's premier computer-aided design software. This is not an architecture in which you can cover up mistakes with wallboard, or in which you can change something part way through because you decide it isn't working. My impression of this style of architecture is that planning is paramount, and after the assembly of the primary support posts and beams, what you do is unchangeable."

While almost all major construction jobs utilize such schedules, at this writing smaller contractors generally don't. East Wind has found the approach essential and uses a schedule on all jobs, even little ones. It took five men, not counting subcontractors, six and a half months to complete the on-site construction, a statistic that reflects the meticulous work required. The preceding shop work took a little more than four months.

FOUNDATION

The first task on the site schedule was pouring the concrete foundations, which East Wind designed in consultation with structural engineers. There are essentially three types of foundation and structural systems used to support Japanese houses today. An East Wind Japanese house often uses a mix of the three systems: stones to support exterior *engawa* posts, hidden stem walls to support the main structure, and a slab in the entryway at ground level. Two of these systems were employed for the guesthouse. Within these systems there are a variety of forms and combinations, but to mention them all is beyond the scope of this book.

Stone-Supported Structures

This is the most picturesque and, to enthusiasts of classical Japanese architecture, surely the most familiar form, since it is seen everywhere in very old structures in Japan. In this system, each post rests on a large foundation stone, set upon more stones that have been pounded in multiple layers into a deep hole. However, packed stone is rarely used now. Instead concrete—instant stone—is used to support natural or milled stones that are tied into a steel reinforcing grade beam, usually 18 inches wide by 24 inches deep, buried in the ground. The arrangement is designed to keep the posts at least six inches away from the soil.

Whether sitting on milled or natural stone, the foot of each post is shaped to precisely fit the stone's contours, and the post is either connected to the stone directly or to the underlying grade beam with a threaded rod or a bolt, which passes through the stone into the concrete.

In order to prevent moisture from entering the bottom surface of the post, a sheet of copper is placed between the post and the supporting stone or concrete. Since copper corrodes with time, it provides the additional benefit of infusing chemicals into the wood that are poisonous to insects and deter rot.

Next, a sizeable wooden beam called a *kamachi* is installed to span the distance between the posts at a height of 18 to 24 inches above grade and is joined to them by mortise and tenon. This beam, approximately 5 inches wide and 10 inches deep, supports the floor, the walls, and any doors. The *kamachi* is usually visible and runs along the finished edge of raised floors and along the outside of most *engawas*. (The floor generally does not actually rest on top of the *kamachi*; floor joists are mortised into the *kamachi's* inside surface below floor level.) Multiple *kamachi* were used in the guesthouse meditation wing to support the room's raised tatami floor and the raised *engawa*.

If the *kamachi* is more than six feet long, it will have its own short posts, called *kento tsuka*, for additional support in the middle of its span. These *kento tsuka* are also supported on smaller stones. If the span is great, girders (*obiki*) resting on their own *kento tsuka* under the floor will add additional

Traditionally, posts were fit to stones to remove them from the ground's dampness. Today a bolt, embedded in wet concrete hidden below grade, goes through the stone into the post. In this house in the mountains, a post on a stone supports the *kamachi*, which serves as a sill for the structure's glass doors.

strength if necessary. Today East Wind has found that conventional floor-joist systems using joist hangers to hold 2 x 6, 2 x 8, or 2 x 10 joists suffice and save time and money, even though the older Japanese system using *obiki* is employed on occasion.

Stem Wall-Supported Structures

This concrete foundation, common for houses in the West, isn't particularly attractive, but it is very strong. Of course, since concrete is a recent invention, it wasn't used for the Japanese houses of old. A stem wall is a short wall, between 12 and 24 inches high, built over a spread foundation 12 to 18 inches wide and 12 to 24 inches deep, laced with steel reinforcing that acts like a grade beam. In many places in California, where seismic activity combines with unstable soils or where steep slopes make engineering a foundation particularly difficult, caissons must be drilled deep into underlying rock or subsoil. The caissons are filled with heavily reinforced concrete to act like the pilings of a pier so the stem walls can be tied to them to support the main interior roof, floors, and wall structures. These concrete walls are usually not visible on the exterior since they are con-

Assembly begins by affixing sills (*dodai*) to slab. Coding on dovetail indicates piece's position and orientation in the structure. A post, cut with female dovetails, will drop onto these sills. The protective plywood on top of the *dodai* will be removed later.

In some instances the ground sill is visible from the exterior, so it is made of finer wood. The cottage's concrete slab foundation was concealed with granite tiles, chosen in black to make the house appear lower and honed to achieve a muted effect.

cealed by the walls of the perimeter *engawas* and lean-tos, whose posts are supported by the more aesthetic stones described above. When stem walls are used for exterior walls, as in the West, they give a "blocky" look to the house and they must be finished in some way.

A *dodai* (sill) about the same size as a post runs along the top of the stem wall and is bolted to the concrete about every four feet. This beam runs *under the posts* and differs from the *kamachi*, which is the beam *attached partway up the posts*. The posts are joined directly to the *dodai*, which is much larger than the 2 x 4 sill plates used in conventional houses in order to provide a solid base for the mortise-and-tenon joints needed. Sometimes the posts are bolted right through the *dodai* to the underlying concrete, which may be required by Western engineers for structural reasons. Since traditional Japanese joints have not been subjected to rigorous evaluation by testing agencies in the United States (an expensive and time-consuming undertaking), the engineering values necessary to demonstrate scientifically the strength of the joinery aren't available to East Wind's engineers. Consequently East Wind and its structural engineers rely upon stud-wall structures to give their buildings the engineering needed to pass uniform building code structural requirements. Since these types of walls are familiar to American engineers and building departments, they are easily engineered to everyone's satisfaction. In all likelihood, the additional strength the joinery adds to the buildings, which isn't calculated, makes these buildings extra strong.

A lower grade of Port Orford cedar is used for the *dodai* than for the *kamachi*, since it usually will not be seen. However, the guesthouse is an exception, since the *dodai* are visible on the exterior of the meditation wing, the raised *engawa*, and the entry. The *dodai* are cherry in the entry, since the finish floor was originally going to be cherry and the *dodai* were planned to match. Elsewhere in the house they are Port Orford cedar.

Floors with short spans are supported by connecting them directly to the *dodai* using joist hangers as described above in discussing the *kamachi*. If the floor spans are large, then sometimes TJIs (trusses made with plywood) or very wide floor joists like 2 x 12s are used, in which case they will be supported by a steel angle iron bolted to the side of the stem wall under the floor. East Wind usually rabbets the interior top edge of the *dodai* so that a 3/4-inch plywood subfloor fits into it and is flush with its top surface, ready for *tatami* or conventional wooden flooring.

Sometimes a layer of copper or aluminum is also placed between the *dodai* and the concrete to prevent termite infestation if the concrete cracks and gives them entry.

Slab-Supported Structures

Site restrictions and planning requirements dictated that the guesthouse have a low profile, so it was built on a slab foundation, which is used to keep a building or a room close to the ground. Rooms where shoes can be worn with easy access from the outside—for example, the kitchen, a living room with furniture, and almost always the entryway, where shoes are left—are generally close to the ground.

Doug Tweed, East Wind's project manager for this particular construction, spent many days working with Morris Stoumen, a trusted concrete contractor to form the concrete and position the hold-down bolts within it. Since the guesthouse, like all traditional Japanese buildings, has very thin walls, positioning the hold-downs inside the walls where they couldn't be

At this home, the elevated Japanese ground sill rests on a stem-wall foundation, which supports the building. Usually, the *engawa*, the distinctive wrap-around veranda common in this architecture, hides the stem wall.

seen was tricky. The walls, which are discussed in depth in chapter 6, have a two-inch cavity between the interior plasterboard and the exterior plywood. The hold-down bolts had to be placed in the wet concrete in alignment with this small cavity before the sills were in place. Since the hold-downs are $1^7/8$-inches wide, there wasn't much room for error. They had to be tight against the posts, too, so they could be tied directly to the foundation.

Usually the top of the slab is about six inches off the ground. Posts and *dodai* are bolted to the slab around the perimeter of the house and between many of the interior posts, just as is done with the stem wall, with the same precautions taken to block termites. In preparation for the hydronic heating, furring was applied on top of the slab, and insulation placed between the furring strips. CDX plywood was then installed across the furring. This was topped with the hydronic heating board, about $3/4$-inch thick, covered with aluminum foil, installed flush with the top of the *dodai*. The heating board came with grooves to receive the heating tubes, which would receive hot water to heat the house. The finish floor was installed over the heating board with a thin foam pad between the two and its edges resting over the *dodai*. In the entryway, the granite slab floor was set directly onto the concrete that had been poured around the heating tubes, making the *dodai* visible inside as well as outside the house.

Ventilation

In a stem-wall system, ventilation is critical to a long-lasting structure. East Wind covers the soil under a raised floor with a polyethylene sheet tightly connected to the concrete walls to prevent moisture from migrating up through the soil and rotting the wooden structures. Ventilation openings must be left in the walls to allow airflow to keep the interior dry, and they have to be screened to keep the critters out.

With a slab foundation, a water barrier of polyethylene sheeting is always placed on the ground and the slab is poured directly over it. Sometimes insulation is added as well. This makes the slab a thermal mass, absorbing excess heat in the heat of the day and radiating heat during the cooler nights.

A polyethylene sheet isn't usually necessary with the post-to-stone type foundation, since ventilation underneath the floor generally isn't a problem unless the area is contained and airflow is restricted. However, most building departments frown upon open spaces below houses, particularly where fire is a concern. If a fireproof barrier is required, then the traditional post-to-stone form must be ventilated and a sheet must be used to keep moisture from being trapped below the floor.

Finally, the construction of the cottage was ready to move into its next phase—one where the fruits of the team's work would become rapidly evident. After months of preparation, the time had come to enjoy the climax of assembling the timber frame.

RAISING THE FRAMEWORK

The crew of carpenters tended to roll into the site about 7:00 A.M., eager to start work. Since the site was four hours from the shop, they were staying nearby at a rented apartment for the duration of the job. Construction couldn't legally begin before 8:00 A.M. or continue after 6:00 P.M., so the men would tiptoe around until 8:00 and then turn everything on at once. Although scheduled to leave at 5:30, they rarely left before 6:00 or 7:00, again tiptoeing and whispering so as not to disturb the neighbors, who in the end marveled that the work had been so quiet. Brian's own reaction: "This was great! It is quieter than Western construction because so much work is done off-site. The actual on-site time seemed very short to me!"

The team's work ethic isn't surprising. A special kind of person is drawn to this kind of construction, and its compelling nature is particularly demonstrated at the site. The men realize that they are making something beautiful, and they don't want to quit. Frequently Brian would arrive after his workday and invite everyone out for dinner, which intensified the crew's resolve to do their very best. They were scrupulous about not wasting time or money, and constantly did little things that weren't in the plans, but which improved the level of the work. Brian says that sometimes he would help them clean up at the end of the day, occasionally vacuuming wood shavings: "It made me feel close to the process."

Posts

The first step in raising the framework was erecting the posts. Each post was positioned right side up near its intended location, with the identification code facing the entryway side. Any ties, like *kamachi* joining posts near ground level, had already been attached to them, because those connections couldn't be made once the posts were in. The post tenons were inserted into the waiting mortises and the posts were slammed down with a thirty-pound oak mallet called a "commander," swung with great force to make the joints tight. A "striker pad," a piece of red elm, was used to protect the finish of the components from the repeated blows. Once together, they fit so tightly they seem to be welded, and only prying tools could have separated

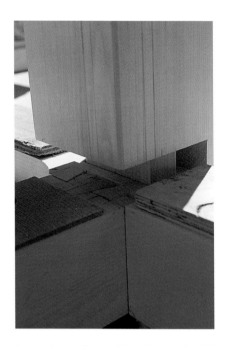

A post tenon being driven into a *dodai* is almost home. Strong, intricate joinery connects all components of the framework without the use of bolts, screws, nails, or adhesives.

them—if they could be separated at all. The last resort for separating them is a hydraulic jack. Even then, separating will usually damage the finishes or even the joints themselves. Once, while building a house in Hawaii, a post with a notch cut into its interior face to receive a ceiling molding was stepped backwards on a sill, the notch on the exterior face. (The coding was facing away from the entryway side of the building). No one noticed until the *keta*—the massive perimeter beam—was not only installed but the post tenon had been wedged in place. The *keta*, 10 feet above the sill, had to be removed, so in came the car jacks, which were positioned underneath the beam. After ruining one jack by stripping its threads and snapping two Douglas fir 2 x 4s, two more hydraulic jacks and two Douglas fir 4 x 4s were found. Using them, the team succeeded in pushing the *keta* up about an inch and a half so they could saw off most of the tenon and turn the post around. A long lag bolt had to substitute for the shortened tenon. The process took about four hours and three men, who continuously muttered about how much more attentive they would be next time.

Installing all the posts for a house usually takes about four hours, but it took considerably longer for the guesthouse. Usually all posts sit on top of the *dodai*, but it was decided that the corner posts should rest directly on the concrete slab rather than on the *dodai*. As a result, the *dodai* had to be connected to the sides of the posts, which meant the use of male dovetails in the ends of the *dodai*. This took extra time, since these joints aren't very strong and generally don't make a clean and tight connection, and they had to be carefully adjusted for a tight fit. But since the wall structure was so substantial, it could also be counted upon to reinforce this connection.

Since extra large timbers weren't used in the guesthouse, there was no need for a crane or other heavy lifting machinery to raise them. This is the case for most houses. A stove lift, however, was borrowed for a few days from a local tool rental company. It is essentially a portable forklift on two small wheels that can hold up to five hundred pounds. A hand crank can lift the loads about 15 feet, more than adequate in this case.

There was no need to put in a sub floor at this point, since the concrete slab was nearly as high as the *dodai* and served as a place to work until much later in the construction process, when the floors were installed.

Beams

The next elements to be installed were the *keta* and the *hari*— the transverse log beams that span rooms and support the roof. But before the *keta* were hoisted into place, they were placed on horses and turned upside down to

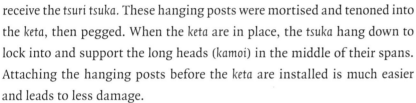

receive the *tsuri tsuka*. These hanging posts were mortised and tenoned into the *keta*, then pegged. When the *keta* are in place, the *tsuka* hang down to lock into and support the long heads (*kamoi*) in the middle of their spans. Attaching the hanging posts before the *keta* are installed is much easier and leads to less damage.

In some buildings where ceilings are used, there is little need for final cutting of components, but in the cottage, where most of the work was visible from the interior and was actually finish work, some pieces needed a bit of trimming or other adjustment. Before installation, the ends of beams fitting into housings are "killed"—that is, made slightly smaller by carefully "bruising" them with a traditional Japanese hammer called a *genno*, which has a blunt and slightly rounded end that doesn't leave hammer tracks or dents. A tight-fitting piece can then be inserted without damage. (The *genno* also has a flat end for use with chisels and for driving nails.) In a day or so, the "killed" wood swells to its original form, expanding within its pocket to make a perfect fit. This is the culmination of the carpenters' skill in laying out, cutting, and finish-planing the joinery. If the layout is wrong, there's a bad fit; if the cutout in either the female or the male pieces is sloppy, there's a bad fit; and if in the finish-planing process the carpenters take off too much, there will be a bad fit. Each process had to be done perfectly—and in most cases it was. Any adjustments involved slightly enlarging the housing (by perhaps $1/64$ inch) or giving a stroke or two with a finish plane, removing only a few thousandths of an inch to create the perfect fit.

Above left: Post-and-beam framework, prepared in the shop, comes together on site. Sugar pine *keta* are dropped into Port Orford cedar posts.

Above: Adjusting mortise of post to receive tenon of waiting log beam.

Above: After the basic frame (composed of *dodai*, posts, *keta* and *hari*) is assembled, the *tsuka* (king and queen posts) are driven in with considerable force.

Above right: Tapered dovetail of a natural log beam is about to be pounded into matching female dovetail in perimeter beam. Pieces are still protectively wrapped from the shop.

To ensure a reliable joint when big logs are involved, final cuts for exact angles and dimensions are made just before installation rather than in the shop, since humidity level at a site is frequently different from at the shop and the logs tend to move a good bit. Once in place, if the logs are dry (and with rare exceptions they are), the fit should be good for a couple of hundred years.

Since the joinery was tight enough to stand erect without wobbling, bracing wasn't necessary as the framework took shape. Once all the *keta* and *hari* were in place, the skeleton was checked to see if it was plumb and square. A plumb bob was employed to check the posts for vertical trueness. If the building isn't perfectly square and plumb, installing the roof will lock the building permanently into a nonsquare form and the roof, which is also precisely cut, won't fit properly. Hip rafters won't come together where they should, rafters won't align at the ridges, and all kinds of troubles ensue.

Sometimes the posts can be slightly out of perfect plumb, but usually by no more than $^1/_8$ inch. Since the posts, once installed, are part of a unit linked together at the base with the *dodai* and at the top by *ketas*, making an adjustment in the plumb of one will bring them all into line simultaneously. To do this, a small hand-operated winch called a "come-along" is used that can exert two to three thousand pounds of force. Once it is determined which direction the tops of the posts have to be moved to bring them into perfect vertical alignment with their bases, the come-along's $^1/_4$-inch aircraft cable is strung between the base of a post and the top of another. The cable is fastened to the post with a wide nylon web to prevent the finishes from being damaged by the force exerted. Tension is applied until the cable is nearly as taught as a guitar string. Once the plumb bob reports success, temporary bracing in the form of 2 x 6s or 2 x 4s is nailed into place at the tops and bottoms of the posts. When the braces are removed, the plywood walls hide the nail holes and preserve the plumb. There is no better way to understand the remarkable lateral strength of all these joints working together than to witness the great force it takes to produce a minute amount of movement.

When the framework is assembled and before purlins, ridges, hips, or rafters are applied, the building's plumb is checked.

Protection of Finished Components and Assemblies

Since Japanese construction calls for the visibility of the structural framework of the finished house, both outside and inside, the next step after raising the framework was to protect the posts from physical damage and sunlight during the rest of the construction. The traditional Japanese carpenter used *tonoko*, a fine whitish clay mixed with water that was painted onto the wood to absorb dirt, oil, and fingerprints. It could be washed off with clear water when the building was done. On top of this *tonoko*, Japanese glue (*nori*) was used to plaster a thin paper to the lumber. Neither *tonoko* nor *nori* is available in the United States, so on the first house Brackett built (his own), he tried using porcelain clay and wallpaper paste to apply paper. The results were mixed. This superfine clay was too fine for the purpose, and the wallpaper paste made too strong a bond, so that neither came off easily, if at all. White porcelain blushes and remnants of paper and glue are still visible here and there where they refuse to let go twenty-eight years later!

Fingerprints left during construction are almost impossible to remove, while the fingerprints of occupants once the house is finished don't seem to be much of a problem. Brackett thinks the difference is that the carpenters are always sharpening and handling tools that are well oiled with camellia oil. The combination of microscopic iron and oil produces fingerprints that won't come out with scrubbing but must be planed out. As a result, the carpenters wear white cotton gloves or wipe their hands on a wet towel hanging from their tool belts as they do much of the work.

Even though many of the components are installed still wearing their wrappings from the shop, neither paper nor plastic wrap are much protection against the inevitable mars, dings, and dents produced on-site—a dangling tool belt nicks a post, a ladder tips over, someone moves a piece of lumber and bangs a door head—no matter how careful and conscientious the carpenters. A different kind of protection is necessary at this stage, and a good solution came from the practice of sawmills, which put very heavy cardboard corners on their lumber going to market to protect it from damage by the steel banding that binds it into groups. Brackett finds that these corners are ideal for covering posts, heads, sills, and other vulnerable components. The cardboard is very tough, comes in six-foot and longer lengths, is relatively inexpensive, and is formed in ninety-degree angles. Each side of the cardboard is about three inches wide and, when taped over both corners of a post, will overlap to protect the entire face. The corners are easily removed to allow work to be done, and they are just as easily replaced.

Benefits of Timber Frames

Two terms are used to describe buildings that use posts to support beams that in turn support the roof. "Post and beam" is a generic term for this kind of building no matter how it is held together—whether by wooden joints, nails, pre-made metal fasteners, steel plates, clips, screws, or bolts. "Timber frame" refers specifically only to post-and-beam structures that are held together with wooden joints.

Jointed wood-frame buildings are not unique to Japan; they have been common worldwide for thousands of years and have significant benefits. Because the joinery is so tight, the building is able to endure an earthquake and spring back to its original form, much the way a modern high rise moves in response to the same stresses. In a sense the building is flexible, though not so flexible that it falls apart. These connections, each individually strong, reinforce each other, so the entire building can absorb terrific shocks as a unit. Brackett reports, "There are two-hundred-year-old houses all over Japan that are in relatively good shape. After two hundred years of earthquakes and typhoons they are still there, still proudly upright, still square and plumb."

While earthquakes have damaged Japanese population centers through the ages, it is not so much because buildings collapsed, but because the tremors often unleashed fires from cooking and heating facilities that raged through cities. The 1995 Kobe earthquake, although devastating, also demonstrated the durability of the traditional architecture. The portion of the city that was destroyed had buildings that were built hastily and inexpensively after World War II on landfill, which acts like gelatin in an earthquake. Prewar buildings that were constructed in the time-proven tradition on solid sites were largely undamaged. Advocates of Japanese joinery often point to Horyuji Temple of Nara, built in 711. Its ninety-foot pagoda has withstood earthquakes and typhoons for almost thirteen centuries.

Most important, joints are made of one of the longest-lasting building materials there is—wood. If wood doesn't burn and is kept dry and protected from termites, it will endure for thousands of years—outlasting Portland concrete by a considerable margin. If carefully jointed, wood continues its normal habit of shrinking and swelling and won't crack or collapse. Deep cracks, of course, weaken wooden timbers, but if checking is going to occur it usually takes place when the wood is curing.

"The cost-per-year of the Japanese house, over several hundred years, is much less than a cheaply built house," Brackett asserts, "not only in terms of the environment, but also for the family that owns and maintains it. Of course, now most people don't think in those terms. Houses used to be built for successive generations of a family, while today, who knows where

Post-and-beam construction allows wide openings to the outside. Since posts support the roof, the space between them can be used for doors rather than load-bearing walls.

a family will reside in thirty years, not to mention two or three hundred! Still, building this way suggests hope for family continuity."

Brian concurs. "This is the first house I've built, and the construction technique is so good that I know it will outlive me. During its construction, the fact of my own mortality hit me very hard. It had to do with the cottage and the *ukiyo-e*. I feel less an owner and more a temporary custodian. It was unnerving and humbling."

Apart from endurance, the timber-frame technique offers a major aesthetic benefit, much like the half-timber construction of England and Northern Europe, since it allows the bold skeleton of the building to be seen. Since the posts hold up the roof, it eliminates the need for the load-bearing walls of stud construction and creates large openings between the posts for doors, windows, and walls. In half-timber construction these openings are generally filled with permanent walls, doors, and windows. In contrast, a Japanese building utilizes sliding panels that can be readily opened to allow access to the garden or to adjacent rooms.

Roof

In assembling Japanese houses there is a constant risk that a heavy rain will spoil the finished lumber while it is still exposed. This risk was intensified in the case of the guesthouse, since the underside of the roof was part of the interior finish. Covering the framework was the next priority. The race was on to get the plywood roof decking completed so that W. R. Grace's construction product, Ice & Water Shield, a self-adhering, rubberized asphalt membrane, could be applied to deflect rain and ultimately act as backup for the final slate and copper roofing. Usually the roofing process takes up to a month; the guesthouse was covered in five weeks, in the exact amount of time scheduled. Had it not been for the complicated roof structure, it could have been done in three weeks.

Various roofing materials had been considered, and slate was chosen because it is extremely durable and very good-looking. At higher elevations, slate is a good choice for its ability to shed snow. Brackett wanted gray or black slate that was flat and not too thick, so that it would accentuate the curves in the roof. In Japan, layers of roofs below the main roof are often clad in interlocking copper shingles, so the lean-to roofs—the connecting roof over the entry and the bath roof—were covered with copper shingles brought from Japan. A rich black slate from Spain was selected that works in unison with the rhythm of the copper shingles.

The Japanese copper shingles were more expensive than the Ameri-

The rich, black Spanish slate chosen for the guesthouse roof should last well over a century.

can product, but they surpassed them in their precision and their elegant detailing for eaves and rakes. Since Brackett believes a house should last for generations, he wants roofs to last too. This particular one should endure for well over a century.

Cameron Brown of C. F. Slating of Fairfax, California, and his crew laid the 10 x 16-inch slate and the copper shingles. The roof deck for copper has to be nearly perfect, without ledges or gaps, since if the roof is walked on the imperfections will "telegraph" with time through the copper and will show a line as the overlying copper bends to fit the less-than-perfectly-flat roof deck below. For most other roofs this isn't a problem. Brown's experienced team included Luther Pahe, widely considered the best slate detailer in the state, and Andreas Ruppin, who achieved Master's Certification in his native Germany in a program that involved everything from mining to marketing. The three were so intrigued by the whole project (it was only the second Japanese house that they had worked on) that they made a trip back when the structure was completely finished to take a look. Cameron reported their reaction in his lilting Scottish brogue: "It's amazing, absolutely beautiful."

Roof Assembly

Once the complex joinery of the frame was assembled, rafters and flat materials like finish roof boards and decking were screwed into place.

Clockwise from top left:

Field rafters are screwed down to purlins. The hammer is being used to knock the piece into alignment.

Eaves blocking and eaves fascia being installed.

Barge rafters give the roof its characteristic Japanese sweep.

Two barge rafters, ridgepole and three purlins in place. The purlins and ridgepole have roof pitch cuts to receive rafters.

Clockwise from top right:

Field and jack rafters installed.

Handsome roof boards of matched-grain Western red cedar are nailed to rafters. The surfaces visible from within will be finish-planed.

Plywood covers roof boards to create a bed for another set of rough rafters. The cavity created will hold insulation and some wiring.

All the lean-to roofs, the small roof over the entryway and the main roof over the bath are roofed with interlocking copper shingles.

Tile roofs color the landscape in Japan and many have lasted a long time, but good-quality slate outlasts even the best high-fired tile, which is very hard, much less available, and about the same price as slate. Most Japanese tiles are low-fired, soft tile that absorbs water. This usually isn't a problem in warmer climates, but when temperatures fall below freezing ice will break up porous tiles.

Insulation

When the roof was covered, the guesthouse was ready for its walls. At this stage a distinct departure had to be made from the construction, but not the appearance, of the traditional wall. The guesthouse had to conform to U.S. building codes, which require rigid or shear walls, particularly in earthquake zones, so East Wind installed studs between the posts, sills, and heads, and then sheathed the outside with plywood and the inside with plasterboard, a gypsum product similar to Sheetrock, to serve as a base for the plaster. The traditional Japanese carpenter forms the walls by building lathwork between the posts and covering it with earthen plaster.

Brackett says, "I have confidence that traditional buildings have the flexible strength to endure lateral loads when the earth shakes them around, but tests on Japanese house design have never been made in the United States, so we have to comply with Western engineering techniques as outlined in the Uniform Building Code." Realistically speaking, there is no way to calculate the shear strength of Japanese joinery or earthen walls without laboratory engineering values, but based on his observations in Japan, Brackett is convinced that these walls and this joinery provide more than adequate strength.

It would be much simpler and cheaper to enclose the outside of the entire structure with plywood or stress-skin panels, but in doing so, the structural elements of the house would also be covered, and the result would be devoid of design interest. Keeping the framework exposed is essential to attaining grace of form.

To preserve the visibility of the framework, the walls were installed *between* the posts and not *over* them, creating what are called infill walls. This results in a relatively thin wall that can't accommodate standard fiberglass insulation, which is important to retain heat in winter and keep the house cool in summer. Lacking insulation, most Japanese homes are drafty and cold in winter. The thin wall, however, can accommodate urethane foam, and since U.S. building code requires insulation of all new houses, Brackett used urethane or isocyanurate foil-covered foam sheets in

The basic bones of the house.

Tsuka, purlins, and ridges added.

Hips and rafters in place.

Studs, some wall plywood, and eaves details in place.

Gables in place over hipped gable roofs, slating is finished and, on the wall closest to the camera, cement board is being applied over two layers of water-resistant paper before plastering.

Copper roof is now complete over entry, the walls ready for plaster, round windows installed.

both the roof and the walls. It is the only insulation that provides adequate R- values for such a thin wall. (R-value indicates the ability of a material to resist heat flow from a warm area to a cooler one. The higher the R-value, the better.) In addition to the insulation, the walls also had to contain the plumbing, electrical wiring, and cables for television and electronic communications.

With the changes of the seasons and relative humidity, the posts inevitably shrink, which can result in water and air infiltration—a problem with all infill walls. Wherever there is a post in a wall plane, there is a break in the waterproof wall, especially if the post is constantly changing dimension, as it will during the seasons. To solve this problem, a flashing for the exterior plywood sheathing was created with a strip of copper about two inches wide fitted into a saw kerf (a very thin circular saw cut) in the surrounding wood members. This allows for the expansion and contraction of structural members while providing a mechanical barrier against drafts and any water that might infiltrate the area between the plaster and the framing. (See Appendix page 198.)

It is also important to properly install vapor barriers in the manner appropriate for the climate. In climates requiring heating and air-conditioning it is crucial to prevent warm, moist air from contacting cold surfaces and condensing. Condensation will produce water in the walls, which will certainly lead to mold, mildew, bacterial growth, and even serious rot. In a moderate climate like that of coastal California, this isn't much of a concern, but since ukiyo-e prints more than a century old were going to be hung on the walls, the possibility of condensation was a prime consideration.

Insulating the roof of the guesthouse's vaulted ceiling was trickier than the walls, because the insulation had to go between the exterior roof deck (the plywood that holds the slate and copper) and the interior finish roof boards. Brackett used rigid foam insulation to achieve maximum insulation with minimum thickness. Its precise thickness depends upon code requirements, climate, and client preference. Because this was a house, not a temple, the roofs were designed to be as simple and as thin as possible. Room for insulation can be provided in three ways, all three of which were utilized for the cottage: (1) Make a convex roof of the type seen on temples, teahouses, and teahouse-style houses. It tapers down to the eaves and was used over the guesthouse entryway. (2) Set the interior finish roof boards and rafters at a different pitch from that of the exterior roof deck. This allows the insulation space to increase between the two planes from the

eaves up to the ridge. This technique was utilized for the lean-to roofs. (3) Keep the rafters of the upper and the lower roof parallel to each other and block out the eaves with a *shin ita*, an eaves board, thereby creating a cavity for insulation. This was the procedure adopted for providing space for the main roof's insulation. (See Appendix pages 200 and 201 for uninsulated and insulated roof sections.)

Insulation work is often subcontracted, but in the case of the guesthouse, the building team installed most of it themselves, including the roof's 2.5-inch-thick isocyanurate foam insulation, which also has a particularly high R-value for its relatively thin profile.

Double-glazed front doors are overlaid with a miniature grid made of recycled wood from a wine cask. Black granite slab floor has radiant heating like the rest of the guesthouse.

Doors

In order to further enclose the structure and protect it from rain and moisture, the sliding glass doors were mounted next. It took East Wind over two decades of experimentation to come up with the Japanese-style, weather-tight, insulated glass doors that were installed in the guesthouse. Traditional Japanese doors and windows don't have weather stripping or double glazing. Most sliding glass doors in Japan today are single-glazed with aluminum framing. It is odd that with all Japan's technical advances, its builders don't seem to have created an attractive, wooden, insulated, sliding glass door in the traditional design. East Wind's doors represent a new American development in their evolution. (See Appendix pages 202 and 203 for detailed sections of the doors, specifications on weather stripping, and suppliers of the necessary components.) A minor but important feature is that each stainless steel double wheel set can be adjusted up or down with a screwdriver while the doors are in place. Precise adjustment to make the doors fit the posts well, move easily, and exert the right amount of compression on the weather stripping used to be very troublesome in the early versions of these sliders, but now it is easy enough for the homeowner to do it himself.

Windows

In selecting the window units, controlling ultraviolet radiation was an important issue, since the organic dyes of the valuable prints are highly susceptible to fading. Custom-designed, double-glazed units were used for both the doors and windows. Each unit consisted of two sheets of glass, a laminated exterior sheet and a tempered interior sheet, the latter coated with LowE Squared, a clear plastic film. (LowE is shorthand for low emissivity.) The laminated glass screens out about 99% of ultraviolet radiation. LowE Squared removes 84% of the remaining 1%, so together they eliminate 99.8% of the damaging rays. LowE Squared also reflects infrared radiation back to its source—back to the house in winter to help keep it warm and back to the exterior in summer to keep it cooler. Drafts are eliminated because the sliding windows abut the posts, jambs, and each other with weather-stripped, tongue-and-groove joints. They are further sealed with brush weather stripping along their tops and bottoms, just like the doors.

Now it was time to move on to completing the interior. More subcontractors began to arrive to provide the crucial technical systems—lighting, heating, plumbing—that would set the guesthouse apart from its antique forebears and make it a viable structure for today's world.

Opposite page: Double-glazed weatherproofed windows have a special coating to block ultraviolet rays that damage art. The ends of the rafters, painted white to block moisture, accentuate the lines of the roof, reminiscent of Buddhist temples. The base of the interior wall is not finish-plastered, since it will be covered when the sleeping platform is installed.

East Wind has modified the traditional *engawa*, the place to sit and enjoy the outdoors. It is raised to chair height in the guesthouse. Shoji panels slide to close the area completely as in a traditional house. (Photo was taken before the sleeping platform was built in the connecting room .)

6 REFINEMENTS

AS THE VARIOUS SUBCONTRACTORS continued to arrive, Brian and Aki watched the cottage take on all the comforts found in new construction today. The modern technical systems, bathing facilities, heating, and appliances blended harmoniously with the classical shoji screens, traditional plaster, and superb woodwork. The subcontractors arrived according to the carefully planned schedule to work for a predetermined number of days.

LIGHTING

Preparations for lighting started in the shop as chases were dadoed into the top of purlins, ridges, and *keta.* These grooves in finished and visible roof structural components hold the wiring and keep it concealed in the finished building. Since the art collection required specialized spotlighting, the lighting consultant, Tom Mourant, recommended large, black fixtures that would harmonize with the door hardware. Brian preferred discreet low-voltage, track lighting and found Translite Sonoma fixtures with small tracks, which would be unobtrusive in the dramatic, exposed roof structure. The decision was finalized when the manufacturer agreed to provide a copper finish to coordinate them with the unlacquered copper detailing elsewhere in the house. They would age gracefully and acquire a patina that would suppress the original bright copper.

The original lighting proposal for the bath called for recessed lighting. Although holes could have been readily made in the woven wood ceiling

Unobtrusive low-voltage track lighting has a copper finish to coordinate with other hardware in the cottage. The purlin's scarf joint is a form of the swallowtail joint.

(shown in the photograph on page 149), Brian wanted it to remain intact, so the next hunt was for appropriate sconces. East Wind was able to recommend a supplier of light fixtures not only for the bath but also for the exterior, where they are placed to light footpaths on all four sides of the house. The manufacturer modified their standard sconce slightly, so that part of the bulb didn't show above the shade. (Further information on all resources and suppliers is found on page 217.)

When assembly started, the electrician, Daniel Flanigan, was on hand to run the wiring at the optimum point in construction. His work couldn't interfere with the carpenters, and the carpenters couldn't advance so far as to complicate his work. The open ceiling required careful timing and inventive solutions to hide the wiring for the extensive lighting system required for the artwork. It was also important that the special harmony of the tokonoma design be discreetly illuminated. Creativity and collaboration were the watchwords in this phase of the construction. The wiring was installed in the roof structure after the purlins and roof structure were assembled but before the finish roof boards went up. More wiring and switching were put in the walls before the insulation and plasterboard were installed, the usual sequence in house construction. Other elements of the electrical system—panels and breakers—were installed at about the same time as the wiring, but the finish electrical work, which involved the installation of switches, the computerized control system, and the fixtures themselves, was one of the last tasks done after the plastering was completed.

A closet in the hallway approaching the Japanese bath became the utility area. Inside it looks like the cockpit of a 747 aircraft, since it holds the seventeen lighting-system transformers, each the size of a toaster, and five computer modules to create lighting "scenes" throughout the house. But that's not all. It also holds the hydronic heating system, with all its digital and plumbing controls as well as the pumps, sensors, and heat exchangers for the hot water supply—all in a three-by-six-foot room! Brian likens it to the engine room of a submarine.

In houses with the traditional dropped wooden ceiling, supplying artificial light is much easier. Recessed can lighting is readily installed. East Wind prefers inconspicuous fixtures, because they detract less from the Japanese finish details. Of course sconce lighting can be mounted on any wall, but Brackett prefers table or floor lamps, which can be moved according to layout or furniture type, and which leave some areas unlit. Shadows that soften lines, creating a feeling of comfort and security, are just as

A basket-weave ceiling in the bath is made with $^1/_{16}$-inch-thick strips of Western red cedar. The Japanese call this kind of weaving *ajiro*. Its flexible construction easily endures a bath's humidity.

important as adequate light. For Brackett, the absence of light is a factor just as important as light, and it, too, should be part of the plan.

Brian also wanted fewer lights than recommended in the lighting consultant's original plan. "We started to ruthlessly delete fixtures," he said. "Especially the exterior sconces, to simplify the lines. That said, I made a mistake. We deleted a track in the meditation wing, which resulted in a really unnatural shadow from an exposed beam on the wall above the round window. Luckily Daniel had recommended that we run the wiring there, just in case we needed a track later. We were also advised to use computer controls with programmable scenes so that the uplighting positioned in the *seiwari* cuts in the *hari* could be turned on separately, to impart a gentle, indirect light. The idea of computer-controlled lighting in such a little cottage seemed outlandish to me, but when Tom explained that we would need a bank of six conventional switches in the gallery simply to control the lighting I wanted, I changed my mind. We chose a system that has a rather inconspicuous, single light-switch panel with soft programmable buttons. I was so glad once the plaster was in that we didn't have to have a large, ugly bank of conventional switches."

HEATING AND COOLING

The guesthouse's hydronic heating system, which silently heats the floor to a maximum of about 75 degrees, is one of the most energy efficient available. The equipment may be costly, but the boiler does double work by also heating tap water and the water for the Japanese bath. Forced air is the most common heating system, especially for houses that have plenty of room above the ceilings or under the floor to run air ducts, but forced air is usually noisy and sometimes doesn't provide even heat. With advance planning, these air ducts can be readily placed under the floor, but for houses built at ground level, this system is probably more trouble than it is worth if it means running ducts underground, below the concrete work. If the house is to be centrally air-conditioned, however, forced air is the only option. (See Appendix page 208.)

In resistance or remote hot water heating systems, registers are embedded in the floor in flat, black metal boxes ten inches deep by about eight inches wide and from two to three feet long. They are covered with removable decorative gratings, made of the same wood as the floor and strong enough to bear foot traffic and furniture. The heat source within the register can be either electric (known as resistance heating), which is very inefficient unless there is a plentiful supply of cheap (renewable) electricity available, or hot water (or some other liquid) delivered to the heater through insulated pipes or tubes from a boiler in a remote location. The hot liquid runs through a radiator, much the same as it does in a car, and heat is transferred into the house. This boiler, like the hydronic heating boiler, can also heat water for the kitchen and bath.

For those who don't mind handling firewood and tending a fire as a part of their daily life, wood stoves are another choice, but stoves and their chimneys are potentially dangerous, so they should be installed carefully according to code requirements and manufacturers' recommendations.

JAPANESE BATH

Aki's traditional Japanese bath is all that she hoped for. It is large enough for two people to enjoy its wraparound garden view. The wooden tub of Port Orford cedar is two feet deep, recessed about twelve inches into the floor with exterior dimensions of thirty-seven by fifty-two inches.

The bathtub and the toilet are in separate rooms, as is the custom in Japan. In traditional Japanese homes the bath may be under the main roof, in a separate wing, or in a shed-roof addition to the main structure. The bathing

Like a decorative scroll on antique furniture, a carved knee brace supports the bathroom windowsill, which is mounted on the outside.

room was finished like a shower stall with waterproof walls and a watertight tile floor with a drain. The bather sits on a low stool and ladles hot water from the tub with a container to pour on his body. After washing, he rinses clean by scooping more hot water from the tub. Dirty water and soapsuds go down the drain in the floor. Then and only then does he enter the tub to soak. This style of bathing keeps the water free from both grime and soap.

Wooden tubs cannot be allowed to dry out or they will shrink and leak. They have to be drained and cleaned with a soft-bristled brush every few days, but without germicidal chemicals, which would damage them. Even with continual care, they will last only about fifteen years. One of the great pleasures of this kind of bath is that the fragrance of the wood is activated by the warm water and permeates the entire house. That is why in Japan a

Guesthouse tub has oil-rubbed, bronze-black fixtures compatible with the Japanese aesthetic. Large waterfall spout fills the tub quickly.

The highly polished sink with contrasting rough edges was carved in China from a single piece of granite.

In another house, the sink has a camphor wood counter and drawer faces. Camphor is frequently used in traditional bathrooms. The luminous transom is a shaving of Western red cedar about 0.004-inch thick, allowing the light behind it to shine through.

tub made of true cypress (maki), with its distinct fragrance, is considered the finest and is the most expensive, although it is not quite as rot-resistant as hinoki. Even if the tub is not made of wood, a similar but less intense fragrance can be produced by making the cover with Port Orford cedar or another cypress. Another alternative is to panel the upper third of the bathing room's walls, beyond the reach of soapy water, with cypress.

Deep Japanese-style tubs that aren't made of wood are also becoming available in the United States, where they are called soaking tubs. Made of acrylic, cast iron, copper, or stainless steel, they don't require the same degree of maintenance as wooden tubs. Tile tubs (ceramic or stone) are also common.

It is easy to err by making a tub too big, forgetting that water volume has a cubic relationship to the dimensions of the tub. Increasing the tub dimensions by seemingly insignificant amounts can increase the water volume enormously, and a large tub is expensive and time-consuming to fill and keep warm.

A dressing room (datsuiba) about six feet square with the same wood floor as the rest of the house is adjacent to the guesthouse bathing room. Its sink was found after an intensive search. "Did we look at sinks!" Brian remembers. "Nothing did much for us. It had to be large, attractive, and correspond in spirit to the aesthetic elements of the rest of the house."

The first idea was to make a freestanding sink, more like a basin set on a vanity top, but the options for plumbing that kind of sink were unappealing. They finally turned to Stone Forest, a manufacturer of Asian-inspired natural stone vessels and light posts. Following East Wind's dimensions, Stone Forest produced a beautiful sink and deck carved in China from a single block of black granite. To the delight of both client and builder, Stone Forest left the sink's exposed edges rough, to contrast with the shiny black finish of the rest. Appropriate bath hardware appeared to be another stumbling block until they discovered Altman's, a company making simple yet striking waterfall faucets with an oil-rubbed, bronze-black finish that was compatible with the hardware in other parts of the house. The tub faucet has a large three-quarter-inch spout that allows the deep tub to be filled, as Brian puts it, "in our lifetime." The dressing area holds linen and bath-supply storage. In some houses, a concealed washer and dryer are installed here.

Here are some points that were considered in the construction of the guesthouse bath. (See Appendix page 204.)

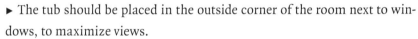

Above: This Port Orford tub in the Sierras is aligned with the windows so the bather has a good view of a creek. However, once constructed Brackett decided the windows were still set too high, and in later designs lowered them in relation to the tub.

Left: Note the compatible heights of tub (12 inches), shelf (8 inches), filling spout, and stool above floor level to make bathing easy. Small bucket is used to scoop warm tub water for washing and rinsing before entering bath.

▶ The tub should be placed in the outside corner of the room next to windows, to maximize views.

▶ The tub should be no deeper than two feet, or the bather will feel trapped and be unable to see outside comfortably.

▶ The windows looking out on the garden should be set so that their bottom rails are below the line of site. This usually means that windowsills adjacent to the tub will be three to six inches below its rim.

▶ Twelve inches above floor level is considered the ideal height for the tub rim. If it's any higher, it's hard to dip hot water from the tub without stretching or standing up. If it's any lower, soapy water may splash into the tub and contaminate the water.

▶ A bar sink faucet with an eight-inch gooseneck can be used to fill the tub, hot and cold if preferred, or cold only if water will be heated in the tub with a recirculating heater. The gooseneck can also be swung outside the tub to fill basins or buckets for bathing or other uses like cleaning.

Deep soaking wooden tubs aren't for everyone. This homeowner prefers to take in the view from a porcelain tub.

▶ A hand-held shower can be mounted on the wall (not over the tub since soapy water shouldn't get into it), with the bottom of the adjustable mast no lower than three or four feet above the floor, so that if it's used as a stand-up shower, the shower head is of sufficient height.

▶ In the bathing area, a shelf about eight inches above the floor and about eight inches deep, usually finished with waterproof tile or stone, is convenient for holding shampoo, razors, and bathing accessories.

▶ If the bathing room is much more than six feet by six feet, it will be harder to heat. More space usually isn't necessary unless the tub is oversized. The guesthouse tub's large dimensions were determined after the house was started, so it is a bit cramped in the six-by-six room.

▶ Care should be taken to seal the floors, and, in cold climates especially, the walls, doors, and ceilings, to keep the moisture from migrating into the rest of the house. When moisture condenses on cold surfaces, it can lead to mold, mildew, and rot. Most Japanese homes have a vent or a window in the bathroom to clear the air of excess moisture.

FLOORING

The specialists for the floating wood floor described in chapter 1 installed five-inch, quarter-sawn planks over the hydronic heating system. No joinery was used to connect the floor joists to the *dodai*, which would have been the usual procedure. When *kamachi* are the means of floor support, nails or Simpson ties are fixed directly to the *kamachi* to hang the floor joists, which support the sub floor on which the finish floor is laid. When the building sits on stem walls, the floor joists rest on ledgers, usually made of steel or aluminum, which are bolted to the concrete stem wall.

The cottage's floating floor was connected only to itself, so that it can move as a unit. When it shrinks, as flooring always does, gaps will not occur between the floorboards. The floor's edges are covered by the walls, door tracks, or sills, which will conceal any shrinkage that may occur in the overall floor unit. The floating floor was supposed to be laid and the baseboards installed before any plastering was done, but because there were unexpected delays in the plumbing work, and because the plasterer was already at the site from Japan, the interior plastering had to be done before the floor was installed. As a result, the floor had to be installed under the plaster, and the baseboards, which usually serve as a plaster ground or solid surface against which plaster is applied, had to be applied on top of the plaster, a very time-consuming and imprecise process. The standard order of tasks is flooring, baseboards, plaster, final electrical and, much later, sanding and finishing of the finish flooring.

Brackett still remembers with great embarrassment a particularly oner-ous floor that he was helping install as an apprentice in Japan: "My teacher, Hide-san, was a man of few words. He usually gave me simple directions. We were building a new temple for Daitokuji, one of the most important Rinzai Zen temples in Japan, and we were in the process of installing the floor of the *tokonoma*. It was in place, but it had to be tightened to the *kama-chi*, its front border.

"In order to tighten it, Hide-san, being much smaller than I, squeezed himself through the ventilation opening under the floor and squirmed about fifty feet to a right turn. He then wormed his way another thirty feet to get under the *tokonoma*—a twenty-minute trip in all.

"Bang, bang, bang.

"'*Tsuita ka?*' (Is it tight?) he called up. I looked. It was still loose, and I told him so. Oddly, he didn't try again or say another word—but again, he wasn't the talkative sort. Twenty minutes passed, and he finally squirmed out from under the floor and went to the *tokonoma*. 'Len, it's loose!' he shouted angrily. I knew that—after all, I'd told him so! I couldn't under-stand why he crawled out without fixing it.

"He crawled under again. Twenty minutes passed, and I heard a shout. He'd run his head into a nail that was sticking through, and I was thinking, 'Oh God, he's going to be in a great mood, now!' '*Tsuita ka?*' he shouted, plainly annoyed with me. 'It's loose!' I shouted back. Another twenty min-utes passed, and out he came again, covered with cobwebs, dust, and with a nasty looking hole in the top of his skull. He went to look at the *tokonoma*, and this time he really got angry. He said it wasn't '*tsuita*,' and I agreed. He was livid. We'd spent more than an hour at this, and still the work wasn't good enough! He looked at me as if I were utterly demented, if not mentally deficient.

"Down he went again, and we went through this process one more time, just like before. He emerged even angrier. I was utterly bewildered, and he thought he was working with a complete idiot. The fourth time he went down he told me to go find something else to do. Obviously I wasn't going to be of any help, and he told me he'd do it himself.

"It was years later that I learned what had happened. The proper way to say 'It's loose' in Japanese is 'Suite iru yo!' My approximation of that was 'Suita yo!'—completely ungrammatical, for one thing, and given the subtle pronunciation difference between *ts* and *s*, easily heard by Hide-san as 'Tsuita yo!' meaning 'It's tight!'

"I don't use either of these words to this day. I find synonyms."

PLASTER

Plaster on wall about to be spread.

The walls were ready for plastering outside and inside with a synthetic substance that imitates all the best qualities of traditional earthen plaster (*jurakudai*). Earthen plaster is nearly impossible to apply well without years of experience, is easily damaged, and can be repaired usually only by re-plastering the entire wall panel. One of the artificial plasters Brackett uses is Julux, a waterproof and weather-resistant plaster made by Shikoku Corporation. Julux is available in several shades, mostly earth colors, and is often partly composed of real soil. It can be applied in a single coat, or a second coat can be added to yield finer results. To the uneducated eye, it looks as good as the traditional clay. Recently this plaster company and others have made available new formulations mixed with straw and soil for even greater similarity to the traditional earthen plaster.

In the process of getting building department approval for the guest-house, East Wind was forced to arrive at a different process for applying plaster that turned out to be an improvement over their former method.

The usual CDX exterior plywood sheathing, $1/2$ or even $3/8$ inch, had been nailed to the studs with its surface set back about $5/8$ inch from the face of the post so the plaster would be slightly recessed. The building department was concerned that the waterproofed mortar coat plus the waterproof exterior plaster finish coat would not keep the plywood sheathing dry. They mandated a waterproof membrane that they were familiar with: two layers of waterproof paper, grade D. But you can't plaster to paper. Applying steel mesh or expanded lath to the paper would have lead to a very thick plaster—too thick to fit inside the posts and still have room for insulation and a reveal (the part to be left visible, that is, the posts). East Wind devised a new procedure that satisfied them: The grade D paper was applied to the plywood, overlapping two-inch wide copper flashings, which penetrated the posts, sills, and the top plates. A $1/4$-inch thick concrete board (Hardibacker) was then put on top of the waterproof paper. Next, a fiber-reinforced base plaster (Dryvit Genesis) was mixed with cement and

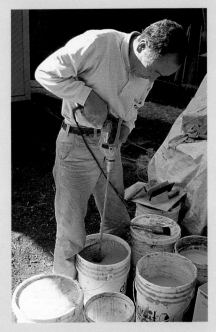

The color of traditional earthen plaster depended on the soil's composition. Man-made plaster allows a choice. Aki Pawlowski chose tan for one room; light green and a darker green for other parts of the cottage.

Plaster for the traditional house was often made from soil taken from the site and mixed with water, straw, and sand. Here, Julux, a commercial plaster designed to mimic earthen plaster, is readied for the guesthouse.

Plaster is kneaded one last time before application to eliminate all lumps and inconsistencies.

Plasterboard is taped using a plastic type mud. Then Plaster Weld is applied to prepare the surface for two coats of interior plaster. Photo shows troweling of the final finish coat.

Final troweling of plaster, after has been allowed to dry slightly, to remove any residual trowel marks.

The afternoon sun burnishes the plaster to a golden hue.

applied as a base coat along with the heavy, eight-ounce nylon mesh that is sold with Dryvit. Finally the finish Japanese exterior plaster was applied with a trowel. (See Appendix page 198.) Two coats were applied to achieve a uniform surface.

Since interior plaster doesn't have to be waterproof or weather resistant, its application was a relatively simple process. It can be applied to almost any gypsum wallboard product, whether plasterboard, Sheetrock, or mortar coat. Both Julux interior and exterior plasters were applied in two coats, using Japanese trowels—which are essential, since they are so thin and flexible. Plastering these materials with anything stiffer inevitably leaves unwanted trowel marks. All gypsum wallboard seams were covered with mesh before plastering, and then they were mudded with Sheetrock tape mud and painted with a chemical bonding agent made by Larsen Products, Plaster-Weld, to ensure that the dried mud wouldn't suck the moisture out of the plaster. In order to preclude subtle differences in texture, all the plaster on any given panel must have the same moisture content. Using dry and stable lumber for the studs and attaching the Sheetrock with galvanized or stainless screws that won't rust and discolor the plaster, rather than nails, further reduces cracking. Bathing rooms generally should not be plastered except high above floor level, and then, only with an exterior plaster, as is commonly done in Japan.

Although some local plasterers in the United States are experienced in working on Japanese-style construction, it was more cost-effective in this instance to bring someone from Japan to apply the finish plaster inside and out. The craftsman East Wind called upon is regarded as one of the best plasterers in Japan, where the Urasenke School of Tea recommends him to builders of ceremonial teahouses. Pawlowski says, "Seeing him work was simply amazing. The other guys on the site would stop and watch him. He used an eight-inch flexible Japanese trowel and achieved incredibly smooth surfaces. Unbelievable. And did he work—starting within one hour of his arrival from Japan. Even more amazing, at the end of the day his tools looked brand new." The plasterer was intrigued by Aki's choice of color for the plaster in the entryway, which he described as "*matcha*," the color of green powdered tea. Aki, a Latin American Studies major, is drawn to the bright colors of South America; from her perspective, she had chosen a subdued color. The meditation room is wrapped in a very subtle light green, the gallery in a faint gray/brown neutral tone that doesn't compete with the art, and the exterior radiates a light earth brown shade to contrast with the dark woods.

The Traditional Mud Wall

Although traditional, earthen walls are now somewhat impractical, they are worth examining for their deceptive simplicity. Mud walls are found in most cultures, but Japanese mud walls are especially labor-intensive to construct and display a perfection of finish rarely seen elsewhere.

The earthen plaster is frequently made from soil taken from the site. The soil's composition has to include some clay. Unfiltered soil is used for the first coat or base wall and is mixed, small stones and all, with three-inch lengths of rice straw (oat hay can also be used) and water. This mixture is left to steep for a couple of weeks before application, to allow the straw to soften and the soil to achieve the right consistency.

Meanwhile a substructure of latticework is erected between the posts of the house. The latticework will receive the earthen plaster in the traditional wattle-and-daub process, a technique common in timber framing around the world. In the half-timber architecture of England, the latticework was composed of a mat of hedge clippings or other small branches woven to form a grid.

The Japanese builder makes a grid of strong wood slats (nuki), $^5/8$ x 5 inches wide, approximately $2^1/2$ to 3 feet on center. He ties two more grids over it, first of stout split-bamboo laths (etsuri) about 1 inch wide, and then of finer split-bamboo strips (shitaji) about $^1/4$-inch wide. (On occasion, builders replace the bamboo with a wooden lath frame.) The fine bamboo pieces are approximately one inch apart in the grid, horizontally and vertically, and are tied together at their intersections with straw rope or sisal twine every two or three inches. While the nuki and the etsuri fit all the way into the surrounding timbers, they stop about $^1/4$-inch short in the lower support sills, where the mortises are intentionally cut deeper than necessary. The shitaji stop about $^1/4$-inch short of all their surrounding timbers. Then, when plaster is applied and its weight pulls down the lath structure a little bit, the grids can sink deeper into their mortises without bottoming out and making the wall bow.

Three different coats of earthen plaster are applied to both sides of the lath. In Japan, the combined thickness of the base coats is about two inches and frequently cracks badly when it dries. The second coat calls for a mixture of sifted soil and shorter pieces of straw, with the addition of sand to prevent cracking. It is important to use 60-mesh sand, which provides the ideal amount of particle surface for proper water adherence. This grade of sand displaces enough water in the mix to prevent the finished surface from cracking later. It is also fine enough so that particles of sand

A home near California's Yuba River has rare, traditional earthen walls made from the reddish soil taken from the site.

won't slough off later when the wall is finished, as coarser sand does. This second coat is about a half inch thick. Two coats are generally considered adequate to produce a fine finish. However, when the second coat dries, a third coat, $^1/_{16}$ to $^1/_8$ -inch thick, can be applied if desired. The third coat is a mixture of fine clay, sand, straw—either dry or presoaked—and a seaweed glue called *nori* that imparts an almost glossy finish. This entire process will finally produce a wall between three and four inches thick.

No reliable recipe can be provided for these mixtures because each soil is different, and the proper proportions of soil, sand, and straw vary significantly as a result. Even if taken from the same source, individual soil samples vary, which is why a professional plasterer familiar with this technique should be called on for high-quality work. Knowing when the plaster mix is right comes only from long experience. Sand and straw are used in proportions sufficient to prevent cracking as the plaster dries, but not in such large amounts that the texture, stickiness, or workability is compromised.

An additional aesthetic touch is sometimes added to interior plaster with a kind of paper wainscoting. Affixed to the lower portion of the wall, the paper—often solid blue or white—adds interest and protects the plaster. Sometimes small iron particles are mixed with interior or exterior plaster coats. They eventually rust, leaving little rust-colored "asterisks" that form a pleasing pattern in the plaster. For added interest, very long straws are sometimes plastered in, one at a time, with the finish coat.

In dense urban settings where houses stand side by side, thick clay walls provide good sound insulation. If multiple layers are applied covering the posts, making soffited eaves with tile roofs, eventually the house became a *kura*—a type of fireproof outbuilding used to store and protect possessions in old Japanese cities, which were always subject to devastating fires. The thickness and mass of earthen walls also explain why the frame of a Japanese house is so strong. The walls of Brackett's own house contain about twenty-five cubic yards—that's two and a half ten-wheel dump trucks—of soil. One large wall may weigh a half ton, about the same as concrete. However, its insulation value, about 2.5 Rs per inch, leaves much to be desired and doesn't conform to energy-conservation requirements since the total R-value for inside and outside, three inches thick, is approximately 7.5, which is considered inadequate by most clients and building codes today.

Because earthen walls eventually hydrate and begin to erode, they are not very durable in places where there is driving rain. To counteract this, they are commonly covered with thin wooden exterior siding to deflect most of the rain. In more sheltered locations, occasional wetting isn't a problem. These walls can absorb remarkable quantities of water, and when the sun emerges after bad weather, steam rises from them as they dry out. In this situation, any noticeable dampness inside the house is rare. A sheltered location is crucial if the traditional plaster, without waterproofing, isn't going to be protected.

Once long ago, East Wind used real soil for the wall of a California house and mixed it with Acryl 60 to make it harder and stickier. It was applied to gypsum wallboard over a base coat of white cement mortar. The result was identical to a traditional real mud wall with all its beauty and complexity—and all its weaknesses as well. Like a traditional wall, it is also nearly impossible to repair.

Just as joinery strength hasn't been measured in the United States, Brackett doesn't believe earthen walls have been tested for shear value (ability to resist lateral loads), but he is convinced that they have a flexible strength that works with traditional joinery *as a building system*, and is part of the reason the buildings endure. In Japan there are many buildings with earthen walls two to four centuries old that appear to be in fine condition.

The Appeal of Natural Materials

As is seen in such components as walls, tatami, shoji, and framework, traditional Japanese house construction places great emphasis on natural materials—straw, clay, paper, and, of course, wood—all available in abundance in Japan. Modern homes today involve so many synthetic and composite materials that the varying uses of natural, unrefined materials have almost been forgotten, as have their methods of application. Except for wooden studs, flooring, and some detailing, the usual building components for most residential buildings today—whether plywood, gypsum board, paint, or glue—are largely manufactured, refined, or ready-to-use. Although natural materials are usually much more complicated to work with, since they lack the uniformity of manufactured ones, they are more interesting for the same reason. Each has its own character. In the traditional architecture of Japan, each post, mud wall, and straw roof is different from the next.

These common materials were so successfully employed that they became integral throughout the entire range of Japanese architecture, from farmhouse to wealthy merchant's mansion to imperial villa. They were beautiful enough even for Japan's aristocratic class, with its highly developed aesthetic sensibility. Applied with an astonishing degree of skill, they led to an aesthetic that focuses on the nature of the materials above all else.

SHOJI

Of all the components of a Japanese house, shoji screens convey a sense of serenity with especial eloquence as they filter light through translucent paper panes, transforming the elements outside to graceful shadows. Lightweight and translucent, they present a delicate counterpoint to the weighty plaster walls.

Shoji were added to the sleeping area of the guesthouse to provide light and privacy. They were installed late in the project, when there was

Shoji silhouettes the stairs in a two-story house. The panes with the X's are double paper panes cut to provide a handhold to open the screen from the outside, a common technique. (Photo by Nicholas King)

little risk of their being damaged or dirtied, and were mounted close to the plane of the glass doors. In a traditional house they are usually found three feet or more from the exterior glass, dividing the *engawa* from the interior, but in this house, lacking the traditional *engawa* corridor, the shoji had to be placed near the glass. The standard post, however, isn't thick enough to act as the jamb for the combined thickness of the shoji and the glass doors, so the shoji were positioned about two inches away from the doors and mounted on their own stand-off frame, composed of top track, bottom track, and jambs. The shoji are precisely fitted to their frames, and since paper is a much better insulator than glass, the two-inch air pocket between them and the exterior doors insulates the room almost as well as an insulated wall.

Shoji first appeared during the Heian period (794–1185), and through the centuries have been mounted in pairs that slide one behind the other in double grooves cut into the wooden members above and below. A six-foot span calls for two shoji, while spans from six to about fifteen feet need four. Anyone who has ever struggled with heavy Western sliding glass doors in metal tracks has to marvel at the utter ease with which these panels move: the push of a finger is enough to send them gliding across their simple, hand-planed wood tracks. East Wind adds small pieces of nylon

Shoji grid pieces of Port Orford cedar are woven basket weave style every two intersections both vertically and horizontally, instead of every one, to minimize breakage of the slender wood during its construction. The standard proportion for panes is usually a ratio of about 2.5 or 3 to 1, with the rectangles generally horizontal.

tape to the screens' bottom corners and sprays a little silicone lubricant in the tracks to make them even easier to move.

Since the shoji can span broad distances and be opened effortlessly, they provide excellent interior ventilation, which is so necessary in the traditional Japanese house because of the high summer heat and humidity. "In winter one can live anywhere, but dwellings unsuited to the hot season are unbearable," declared the thirteenth-century sage Yoshida Kenko in his *Essays in Idleness (Tsurezuregusa).*

East Wind's shoji are 1 bu (about an 1/8 inch) thicker than what is usual in Japan because they are taller to accommodate American homeowners— and also because they are likely to be treated more roughly than in Japan. Very large shoji are seen in the large temples, but in residential architecture they tend to be more or less standard in size.

Brackett prefers to use Port Orford cedar for the grid of thin crosspieces (*kumiko*), since it is unlikely to snap in the slender dimensions required. On occasion he will use Western red cedar or redwood, but these woods are much more prone to breakage. The *kumiko* are generally $^1/_4$ x $^1/_2$ inches, although sometimes they are $^3/_8$ x $^3/_4$ inches, especially for wider shoji.

The shoji's latticework and the frame were prepared together. The vertical and horizontal pieces were "woven" basket-weave style over and under each other. The components were half lapped by twos to receive the intersecting pieces—that is, where the ribs intersect, a half lap joint was cut in the front of the first two crosspieces and in the back of the two matching verticals, making the surfaces of the ribs flush. The next two horizontal pieces were cut on the back, the intersecting verticals on the front.

Shoji can also be woven every other one, rather than every other two, and while it's considered better work, it's tricky. In doing so the shoji maker must make extra crosspieces, since some may break in the weaving process. Weaving by twos reduces the risk of breakage during assembly, yet keeps the grating flat and retains the advantage of alternating laps, which make the entire assembly more resilient in rough use. The lattice is attached to the frame using tiny mortise-and-tenon joints. A wood baseboard (*koshi ita*) is optional; it gives the shoji further strength and stability, and is less likely to be damaged by feet, vacuum cleaners, brooms or other items close to the floor.

By varying the placement of the *kumiko*, shoji can be created in a wide variety of patterns, including complex geometric patterns for special uses. East Wind sometimes also makes a special kind of *yukimi* shoji (snow-viewing shoji), in which half the screen slides up to reveal a built-in window or screen behind, providing protection from cold winds while affording a

Eight shoji and glass sliders partition one wing. View is
from exterior across room to central garden.

Shoji are traditionally placed between the *engawa* and the interior, as is seen in this Colorado building. Bamboo blinds, *sudare*, provide privacy and protect the interior from intense alpine sunlight.

view outside. (See photo on page 41.) The company has devised several methods of installing window screens to keep out insects as well, and also incorporates them into the design of glass doors.

When the frame and lattice are complete, the translucent paper is applied. Contemporary paper made for this purpose has an imperceptible amount of plastic that makes it as strong as the traditional handmade paper used for it called *washi*. And like *washi*, it doesn't yellow. Modern paper comes in three-foot rolls—far wider than *washi*—making it easier to apply, since one piece covers the width of the entire door. This also allows greater versatility in the placement of the *kumiko*.

Washi is often erroneously referred to as "rice paper," but it is usually made from the inner bark of the branches of the mulberry bush, although high-quality *washi* is also produced from the barks of the *mitsumata* and *gampi*, shrubs indigenous to Japan. Like so many of Japan's arts, the techniques have evolved within families dedicated to the craft, and the paper is produced in rural areas where the plants are abundant. *Washi* is so strong that it is even affixed to bamboo frames to make umbrellas. Machine-made papers retain some of the sulfuric acid used in their production to break down the cellulose fibers. Genuine *washi* is acid free and amazingly tough.

Applied to shoji, *washi* is dramatically translucent; it admits as much as fifty percent of the outdoor light. Many sheets of *washi* have beautiful natural patterns of long fibers floating across the surface in texturally rich but muted designs. *Washi* made for shoji comes in two standard widths— approximately 11.25 inches and 9.5 inches, and the shoji grid is usually made to accommodate one of these two sizes. Japanese paper generally has a rough and smooth side; the smooth side should face the exterior so the more interesting matte texture can be seen from within.

The paper is affixed horizontally across the framework with a water-soluble glue made from starch. The guesthouse shoji were papered with Japanese glue (*nori*). Cornstarch or laundry starch is also effective, dissolved in water and cooked to a paste slightly thicker than gravy. The paste is applied using either a special brush made for this process, five or six inches wide with a short $^1/_2$- or $^3/_4$-inch bristle, or with a short-nap paint roller and a paint tray. The guesthouse crew used a paint roller for the most part, but for tricky spots such as the finger-pull openings they employed a brush. Japanese glue and brushes are available from Japanese tool or art supply stores. "Instant" powdered *nori*, which must be mixed with water, is not recommended. It seems to crystallize over time and lose its adhesive qualities, and it picks up the pigments in the wood, staining the paper.

The paper was applied horizontally from the bottom and worked up, with the upper sheet overlapping the lower where they met on the crosspiece, just like roof shingles. The paper covers the full width of both the lower and upper *kumiko* and an area matching their width on the perimeter frame. Though shoji paper is manufactured to fit the framework, in special cases it may have to be trimmed a bit. If so, the paper has to be cut to size prior to application, since repeatedly cutting through the paper and into the frame will eventually mar and ruin the frame. Once the glue dried, the paper was misted lightly with water so that it went taut as it dried.

The shoji's delicate framework and paper panes counterbalance the massive, naturally curved beam of incense cedar in this Northern California home.

The shoji's paper panes provide privacy and effective insulation for this corner reading nook.

In a bedroom, shoji window screens filter the light, allowing the day to start softly. The panels' grids can be made in a variety of decorative patterns.

A tear in the paper can be repaired in a simple and charming manner with a small piece of *washi* cut into a snowflake or flower design and glued over the tear. The Japanese tend to repaper shoji completely as part of the annual New Year's cleaning. The water-soluble glue makes the paper readily removable. Elmer's Glue or any other kind of permanent glue should never be used, as it will be very difficult or impossible to remove cleanly. The first step in repapering is to soften the glue by moistening the old paper where it is attached to the frame. This can be done by dabbing the area with a damp sponge or even by spraying it with water. Let it sit a short while until the glue is soft, and then pull the paper off as cleanly as possible. Use a clean wet cloth to remove all the old glue and pieces of paper, and then wipe down the entire grid to remove dust and dirt. Allow the frame to dry for an hour or two and then apply new glue with either the special brush or a roller.

Shoji evolved from *fusuma*, the solid sliding screens that serve as removable partitions between rooms and are covered on both sides with a heavy, opaque handmade paper or, in more luxurious buildings, silk. These panels, too, slide easily on grooved wooden tracks that are shallow at floor level and deeper above so that the panels can easily be lifted out to make two rooms into one. *Fusuma* frames are often lacquered, the paper becoming a canvas for elaborate paintings. *Fusuma* decorated with rich gold leaf make a functional as well as an artistic contribution, since if they are positioned opposite windows, the gold reflects the natural light and further illuminates the room.

AMADO

Before the invention of glass doors, wooden doors called *amado* ("rain doors") protected the shoji from rain and snow. Glass was not used as a building material to enclose architectural spaces in Japan until the beginning of the twentieth century. The ingenious *amado* have no parallel in contemporary architecture. These thin, relatively light wooden doors or shutters run on a single track and can be pushed completely out of the way, opening the wall completely—unlike sliding glass doors, only half of which can be opened and which are too heavy to be easily removed. When in place across an opening, *amado* lock together, tongue and groove, at their vertical edges for a tight fit that keeps out most of the wind and rain.

Amado are opened by sliding them down the track, one at a time, into a box mounted on the house wall at the end of the opening. The box is wide enough to accommodate the combined thickness of all the panels but it has a slot just large enough to admit a single panel at a time. As the *amado* roll off the rail, which terminates at the box, they stack one beside the other, like books on a bookshelf. They are closed by reaching into an opening in the door slot and pulling out a door. On emerging the door automatically self-aligns with the rail and jumps up onto it, ready to slide into position (see Appendix pages 206 and 207).

When all the *amado* are in place across the expanse, with all their stiles locked together in tongue-and-groove joints, the door closest to the storage box is locked by slipping wooden bolts into both the upper and lower tracks, preventing the removal of any of them.

A California barn is secured with locking shutters, designed like traditional *amado*. All the wood panels slide completely off the window into the end box.

These shutters keep intruders out, protect the inner shoji from most weather damage (even flying debris in a typhoon), and effectively close a house up so that no one can see inside. Since they also block out all exterior light, they are usually only shut when the household retires for the night or the occupants are absent. In more recent construction *amado* have been

In the traditional house, shoji separated the room from the *engawa*, creating a transitional space that can be considered either interior or exterior.

replaced by glass doors—though as mentioned earlier, the quality of sliding glass doors in Japan still leaves much to be desired.

ENGAWA

Finally we come to the *engawa*, the wraparound verandas or corridors mentioned in chapter 1, that are a unique and essential design element of the traditional Japanese house. These verandas gently bring the inside out and the outside in, connecting the Japanese house to the outdoors. The *engawa* provides the occupants an overview of the garden from the interior at an elevation of about a foot and a half, just high enough to see the garden's extent but low enough that one doesn't feel removed from it. The roof overhang and posts frame the view, much the way that a frame enhances a painting. The *engawa* also allows occupants to actually experience the

The *engawa* concept has been modified to become a bay window seat, softened with a futon in a Bay Area bedroom. Bath and dressing room are beyond.

garden by providing a place to sit in it. Its wooden floor is generally about 1 1/4 inches (1 *sun*) below the tatami level. Depending on the floor plan, the *engawa* may also serve as a corridor, connecting the rooms of the house around its perimeter.

Because of the narrow footprint of the guesthouse determined by the lot size, there was no room for a traditional *engawa*. Even if there were room, attaching an *engawa* to a room with furniture creates unbalanced eye levels. (Normally one sits directly on the *engawa* floor, which is too narrow to accommodate furniture.)

For the guesthouse, Brackett provided a small transition space between the interior and exterior that takes a hint from the traditional *engawa*. He built an alcove facing the inner garden, raised to chair height (sixteen inches or slightly less) and covered with tatami. (See Appendix page 209.) In some houses, wedge-shaped foam pillows at the ends make backrests and help turn the space into a cozy reading nook as well. In a pinch, it is even a place for guests to sleep. With sliding glass windows on its outer wall, it is bordered on its inner edge with shoji to separate it from the interior. Children especially love to claim this area as their secret hideaway. Its ceilings can be flat and usually lower than ceilings in the main house, or the roof structure can be finished and left exposed.

Designed to resemble a traditional kitchen *tansu*, the chest in the gallery holds art plus a refrigerator, microwave, a bar sink, and espresso machine.

BUILT-INS

The Kitchen in the Tansu

The final additions to the building were its specialized cabinets. The large chest built to store art and conceal the beverage appliances was custom-made of European elm, similar to the *keyaki* wood often used for *tansu* in Japan. Nine feet wide and nine feet tall, it was built by a former East Wind apprentice, Phil Garcia, who established his own company, 14th Street Millworks in Sacramento, specializing in custom furniture and cabinetry. One of the chest's three interlocking stacked sections has sliding doors covering bays with removable baffles to store framed art. At the top, two sliding wooden doors open to a storage area for large items. The middle portion conceals the small appliances—an espresso machine, a microwave, and a drop-in bar sink with an antique copper patina bowl and a faucet in weathered copper. The lower portion has drawer storage and conceals a small refrigerator/freezer. Provision had to be made in the cabinet design to ensure that heat wouldn't build up from any of the machines. Hot and cold water as well as the waste water had to be plumbed in during its construction and designed so that it could be easily connected to the in-house plumbing.

Kitchens

Many of the houses East Wind makes are primary dwellings, unlike the guesthouse, and have full kitchens filled with the latest appliances and the newest look in counters. Beautiful wood and stone can predominate and still readily accord with contemporary technology, as the photographs of other Japanese homes in the United States demonstrate. Cabinetmakers craft upper and lower cabinets in a Japanese style and accentuate them with hardware used on Japanese chests. Compatible modern hardware is also an option. Appliances are often faced with wood to match the cabinets or are hidden within cabinetry to make the room a warm, harmonious unit.

The complete modern kitchens available in contemporary Japanese houses today are a far cry from the traditional kitchens of folk houses. With compacted earthen floors and open fires, they were smoky, cold, and unin-

Above: An up-to-date, full size, Western kitchen, one with its own little display alcove, looks right at home in a Japanese context.

Left: Another view of the kitchen looking toward eating area.

viting, although their open roof structures or porous bamboo lathwork ceilings that allowed smoke to escape were beautiful. Comfort, convenience, and conviviality were not considerations for traditional kitchens. They usually occupied the coldest, darkest corner of the house and were thought of as a workplace. Now an entirely different attitude toward the kitchen prevails in both Japan and the West. It is regarded as living space, and must be attractive, warm, and airy in addition to being an efficient work space.

Closet/Cupboard

Another of Brackett's innovations is a specially designed closet (*oshiire*) that makes storing a futon easy. The traditional *oshiire*, where the futon is stored every morning, is usually fitted with sliding doors which allow access to only half the closet at a time, making it difficult to get a folded futon into a three-foot opening. Instead of a sliding door, East Wind has given the lower space a flip-up door that runs its entire width, so the futon can be simply slid into a six-foot opening. The horizontal divider between its upper and lower portions makes the lower portion two or two and half

Granite countertops with American cherry (*Prunus serotina*) cabinets and flooring dramatize a thoroughly Western kitchen.

The cabinet, designed by Pawlowski and Shallenberger, is mahogany, considered the best wood for archival storage. It holds 300 prints lying flat in shallow drawers with removable dividers to accommodate single, double, and triple prints. Curvilinear base is sapele; drawer pulls are pear.

feet high, about three feet deep, and six feet or so wide. In the upper half, traditional sliding doors cover built-in shelves, cabinets, or drawers for clothing and personal items. The sliding doors in the upper portion can be recessed back into the opening, leaving an attractive display shelf on which to place a lamp or a flower arrangement.

Furnishings

Custom furniture designer Jefferson Shallenberger was shown the plans for the house and the wood choices to allow him to design specialized furniture that fit within the cottage. In addition to the mahogany print cabinet shown in the photograph, he created a collapsible table with two sets of legs so that it can be used at either standard Western height or as a low tea table for floor sitting. The table sits on the tatami platform in the sleeping area, ready for entertaining. When guests stay the night, it can be stored and a futon spread out on the tatami.

One of the last tasks involved adding door handles and finger pulls. Their positions were determined not by mathematical calculation, but for comfort and convenience. For example, in the sleeping area, the glass

The dining table has another set of longer legs to be used with chairs elsewhere in the cottage. Three pullout drawers, faced with grids and backing of European elm, provide storage. When a guest spends the night, a futon stored in the long open drawer replaces the table.

doors and shoji flanking the raised tatami platform, which are set at the tatami level, have low finger pulls and screw locks so a person lying down can readily open or close them without getting up.

LANDSCAPING

As the project drew to a close, the Pawlowskis explored landscaping at local nurseries. While the structure was designed to focus on the exterior, East Wind leaves the details of the landscaping up to the homeowner. Part of the plantings had to integrate the approach to the cottage with the California landscaping of the backyard immediately behind the main house, which included a lawn, two tall palm trees, and a distinguished old oak. Local Bouquet Canyon stones with tumbled edges to resemble river stones were laid across the lawn in differing sizes to encourage a leisurely pace. As the path approached a Chinese wisteria that partially hid the cottage, it inscribed an "S" shape through the garden's trees to allow the building to come into view slowly. A maple tree partially obscures one of the round windows, as Brian had planned to interrupt the symmetry and to provide

Azaleas and cut-leaf maples, evergreen mainstays of a Japanese garden, enhance the interior courtyard. The back of the cottage is as graceful as the front.

interest when viewing the garden from inside. Nearby is an Akebono flowering cherry (*Prunus x yedoensis* "Akebono") that competes for attention with no fewer than twenty Japanese maples of many varieties. Various species of bamboo were planted along the property line fence to provide further privacy, but the yellow-and-green-striped culms of "Spectabilis" bamboo (*Phyllostachys aureosulcata* "Spectabilis") tended to draw the eye first. *Moso* bamboo (*Phyllostachys pubescens*), the largest of the temperate bamboo, which can reach seventy-five feet, was planted behind the cottage in the owners' private "park" with the ninety-foot pines and redwoods—but not before a heavy plastic barrier was sunk three feet into the ground around it to keep it from taking over the yard.

The courtyard garden between the wings was carefully arranged so that it could be fully appreciated only from the tub. Standing in the bathing room affords a limited view down through the low windows. But the sitting bather is rewarded with a full view of a weeping Tamukeyama maple and a stand of giant black bamboo (*Phyllostachys nigra* "Daikokuchiku").

As completion neared, Brian said, "I've talked with friends who had construction jobs done and they were always stressed out and unhappy. But the men on this job had such a passion for their work. It was unbelievable. East Wind was cool. They were fun to talk to and be with. I'll miss them when they're gone."

The owners are now so pleased with the guesthouse that they have found many ways to use it and are contemplating making it their master bedroom as well. Brian says, "The cottage encourages you to experience it in many ways. One night during a lull in a party, I was sitting in the little reading alcove sipping cold sake from a wooden cup listening to a koto player that we had for the evening. The window was open, it was a mild night, and I could hear the raindrops' counterpoint on the roof. Wonderful sensory immersion—great to see the craftsmanship, touch the wood, enjoy its fragrance, and then hear these sounds. . . ."

Hide Tadayuki, Len's teacher, considered one of the best carpenters in Japan, working on a temple in Kyoto about 1993.

7 ON BEING AN APPRENTICE

AS A RESULT OF HIS UNUSUAL AND valuable apprenticeship in Kyoto, Brackett has some solid advice about getting along in Japan, about learning a skill anywhere, and about becoming a craftsman.

He vividly remembers his reaction thirty years ago when the Zen master Kobori Roshi said, "I can introduce you to the best carpenter in Japan." He was astonished at what he had stumbled into, but he says he was too young and naïve to be intimidated by such an extraordinary introduction. He did not, however, leap at the chance; instead he asked for some time to decide, since he was aware that there were implications of commitment and obligation in accepting, and he wanted to be sure what they were and whether he could fulfill them.

Brackett turned to his brother-in-law, Richard Baker, for advice. Baker was in Kyoto that year, going through the process of being prepared for installation as the abbot of the San Francisco Zen Center.[1] When he asked him, "Exactly who is Kobori Roshi?" he was told that he was a renowned figure who knew almost everybody in Japan who was important, and that if he said he could introduce you to the best carpenter in Japan, he probably could.

Baker gave Brackett five points to think about, which anyone considering being an apprentice in Japan will still find valuable. First, an offer of an apprenticeship, which is a very formal act, is not a compulsory invitation. A delay in deciding is viewed as evidence that it and the ensuing commitments

[1] Baker was abbot of the San Francisco Zen Center from 1971 to 1983. He is presently the abbot of Crestone Mountain Zen Center in Crestone, Colorado.

to the sponsor and the teacher are being thoughtfully considered. If the eventual decision is "Thanks, but no thanks," that is entirely acceptable.

Second, if you do accept, you can't quit; you must see it through or everyone connected with you will suffer. The sponsor will have recommended someone who didn't keep his promises and will lose face. The teacher will have failed to keep an apprentice and he will lose face. And the apprentice will have failed by not following through. Also very important in the equation is that later potential apprentices will have to deal with "the other foreigner's" failures.

Third, don't live with your teacher. If you do, you will be expected to behave as if you were Japanese twenty-four hours a day, but you will never become Japanese. Living with your teacher is extremely stressful and is likely to have unfortunate consequences. It is essential to be able to retreat into one's own culture, to not be on duty all the time. Otherwise there is no rest, and very few foreigners in Japan can last in this situation. Being an apprentice ten to twelve hours a day is stressful enough.

Fourth, do not enter into an apprentice relationship unless there are very clear reasons to expect it to work. As much as possible, you should seek assurance that the teacher is skilled and knowledgeable, and that his reasons for taking on the apprentice are pure. While it is always hard to predict another's personality traits, the choice should be carefully made, since this commitment is like forming a new family tie. A test period will usually not be offered, because that would be considered embarrassing to the teacher and the sponsor.

And fifth, a potential apprentice should spend at least six months or a year in Japan to learn some Japanese and something about the culture first. While living there, you can decide if you even like being in Japan. This is important, because an apprentice will experience traditional Japan to a greater degree than those who merely live there. The world of traditional arts and crafts is extremely structured, and entering it can change not only the way you live but also who you are. "Even though you won't be accepted as a Japanese, you will be expected to play by Japanese rules, and if you don't like Japan or know how things work, you simply won't succeed. It takes most people years to grasp what's really going on, but an awareness of this is important to minimize misunderstandings. Many intercultural gaffs will be forgiven, but it makes sense to know how to avoid some of them anyway."

To the twenty-two-year-old American, the prospect of a five-year commitment loomed as a very long span of time, but after agonizing over the decision, two things became clear to him: accepting an apprenticeship was likely to be one of the most important decisions he'd ever make, and the acceptance would change his life in a very significant way. In the process, he also thought about what else he wanted to do. Continuing his travels would be interesting but probably wouldn't have the impact on him that this offer promised. Essentially it came down to the question, "What else is worth doing?" About the only other thing he could think of was becoming a Zen monk, and that didn't genuinely appeal to him. "Since there was no foreigner I could talk to who had ever done this," recalls Brackett, "I held my nose, closed my eyes, and jumped, not knowing where I would land." It eventually became apparent that he picked the best imaginable place to make that plunge, and that he was very lucky to find himself in the company of some of the finest craftsmen in Japan, who were not only very skilled but also extremely sensitive, kind people. It could have been miserable, and for some who came after him, it has been. But he was fortunate.

The construction company to which Brackett was introduced, Kamiyama Komuten, was very carefully disassembling a magnificent house on Muromachi Street in Kyoto, built in 1605. The area gave its name to an elegant period in Japanese history. In the fourteenth century, the military clan of Takauji Ashikaga took control of the shogunate and moved its headquarters to Kyoto and into the Muromachi district. The subsequent Muromachi period (1338–1573) saw the development of the theatrical arts of No and Kyogen, flower arranging, ink painting, and the tea ceremony, with its triumph of architectural simplicity, the teahouse. In time, the district became known for its silk merchants, whose shimmering bolts were a precious commodity that eventually made the merchant class wealthy and powerful.

The construction team was dismantling the house of a silk-merchant family that had been built at a time of remarkable wealth and aesthetic sophistication. They were intent on salvaging the priceless building materials, such as rare old-growth cedar ceilings, ebony *engawa* planks twelve inches wide and twenty feet long, and priceless decorative transoms and screens. Brackett's teacher, the head carpenter, was indeed one of the best carpenters in Japan—a man just as skilled at building temples as teahouses, which are rarely done by the same craftsman. He told Len, "Pay attention. This building is the best there is." It was step one in what the West now calls reverse engineering. What better way to understand the best work than to take it apart, piece by piece!

"When we began removing the ceiling boards, six inches of dust, the accumulation of almost four centuries, came cascading down on me. By the end of the day my face was absolutely black with soot. Returning to the public bath in the small village where I lived, my fellow bathers privately wondered who this lunatic was. Finally one asked very politely why I was *so* dirty every day. From that day on, they greeted me approvingly whenever I came into the bath."

The team moved on to Ohara, a village northeast of Kyoto, to spend three years building a new temple on an ancient site—Shobo-an. All new lumber had to be prepared so that it was flat, straight, square, and of uniform dimension, a task normally accomplished with a jointer and a thickness planer. These machines were located at the company's shop in Kyoto, far from the remote location of the temple. Some of the lumber was milled in the shop, but a lot of it was given to Brackett to mill with a hand plane on site, a process that took about two years. In retrospect he realizes that they created the assignment for him, since such work was a rare opportunity in the machine age, even if he didn't understand that at the time.

In Japan, the relationship between teacher and apprentice is formal, sometimes even harsh; it isn't a friendship, even if bonds of affection develop over time. Instruction is not planned. The teacher doesn't take the apprentice aside and give lessons. One has to teach oneself, by watching and trying to emulate skilled craftsmen. As Brackett expresses it, "You have to steal knowledge from your teacher." Questions about construction or architectural design not relevant to the work at hand are not in order during work hours, but may be asked during lunch or a tea break. Sometimes the response is that the apprentice needs to wait to ask the question until he knows more and will be able to understand the answer.

The apprentice is expected to accomplish the task exactly as instructed or incur severe displeasure. Brackett explains that the apprenticeship system works well in Japan's hierarchical society, where people are accustomed to accepting the restrictions of their rank. The apprentice is at the bottom of the ladder, deferential to the teacher and apprehensive about making a mistake. While this "fear" of the teacher is something that Westerners might find objectionable, there is no question that a little anxiety is helpful in keeping the apprentice alert and receptive to learning. Of course it is essential in the West as well as in Japan that the teacher not let his own demons pollute the relationship. Taking out one's frustrations on apprentices endangers a rare and remarkable relationship, but at the same time severity is sometimes necessary.

Brackett once mentioned to his sister that he owed a lot to his teachers, and she shot back, "You owe your life to your teachers, Len!" He said, "That set me back on my heels, as it should have! I was nonchalant about having received such a gift. I *do* owe my life to my teachers, to all my teachers—my parents, my friends, my teachers in school, my carpentry teachers, my Zen teachers—to anyone who took my interests to heart, and even to those who didn't. Even being subjected to cruelties and bad behavior is to receive a kind of teaching.

"But I was also taught in indirect ways. Occasionally my teacher and I would drive together to work in Ohara, and one day on our way back he said he wanted me to meet someone. We went down a small street to an opening in a wall and in we went. Inside was an old woman who was a silk weaver. I was astounded at the beauty of the obi she was weaving. The sash was about eight feet long and a foot wide. The warp of the loom looked like spider's webs with thousands of threads. Her fingernails were filed to serrated edges to allow her to push the threads on the loom tight. I asked her how long this work had taken, and she told me that she had four months left on it, but that she'd been at work for the last year and a half! I remember being so moved at the effort people make to create very beautiful things."

Years later, Brackett returned to Japan with his wife, Toshiko, and visited the man responsible for launching his career. Kobori Roshi was near death, but he made one request of the former apprentice. He told Len that he was in a position to "take to America the best Japan has to offer," not only its architecture, but also "the way a person has to be" to do this kind of architecture. Kobori Roshi was dismayed that Americans often thought of Japan in terms of electronic gadgets and toys, when its architectural tradition was far more significant. He reminded Len that just as he had been taken in hand and taught, he now had a responsibility to teach as well.

For more than twenty years, Brackett has been trying to put this classical architecture into an American context. He aspires to improve the life of his clients, his staff, and his apprentices by remaining true to the skills and standards of his teachers and sponsors. But teaching an apprentice isn't as easy in the United States as it is in Japan. Brackett says, "Since democratic principles are part of our very psyche, and we are all considered equal, Americans are more likely to do what they think is right for them and not surrender themselves to a teacher as readily as a Japanese apprentice. Of course, surrendering oneself to anyone, irrevocably, probably isn't ever a good idea, but there is *so much to learn*. This is, after all, a cumulative body of knowledge and it isn't likely that anyone will stumble upon certain basic techniques without guidance. It is important for the student to relinquish the idea that he knows anything and simply listen to whoever knows it well and do what he is told, especially for the first two or three years.

"My teacher used to tell me how to live my life, too, and at the age I was then, I wasn't very receptive to his injunctions. I see now what he meant. For me to become a craftsman I had to learn a lot more than just how to use tools; I had to redo everything. I had to learn a new way to be. In the United States workers don't sign on for life, either to a company or to a profession, while in Japan, your occupation is a major part of your identity. When you say, 'I am a temple carpenter,' you are doing more than telling someone what your job is. For that individual, 'I am a temple carpenter' means 'every thread of my existence is temple carpenter. I think like a craftsman, my soul is craftsman, I am a craftsman to my core, and everything I do is done that way, whether it's cleaning the shop, tying my shoes, or writing a letter.'"

For this kind of craftsman, family and leisurely pursuits are necessarily secondary to work, especially in the early years In the years of Brackett's apprenticeship in Japan and for many years after his return to the United States, he had no leisure-time activities. The work was so compelling that it consumed all his energies.

Today Brackett gets one or two inquiries a month from young men who would like to become his apprentice. He finds that frequently they have unrealistic ideas about what's involved and are expecting Japanese carpentry to be an exercise in calming oneself, imagining a kind of carpenter-meditation. He says, "To a certain degree, it is meditative, especially when one isn't the head carpenter, but mostly it isn't. Japanese carpentry requires considerable intellectual involvement. It's complicated. And the young men don't understand that an apprenticeship is both an emotional and economic relationship. It isn't all magic. A lot of being an apprentice is just stacking lumber or going to work every day when you don't want to."

Brackett recognizes that Americans have lives outside of work and that they are not accustomed to making five-year commitments, but he feels five years are absolutely necessary to learn the basics. Even so, both in the United States and in Japan, there are apprentices who don't stay the full term. The study of temple carpentry generally takes another ten years. In

Western culture, where so much value is placed on individual freedom and there isn't acute social pressure to fit into a certain social niche, the prospect of apprenticeship, with its lengthy investment of time and proscriptions on personal freedom, is not highly valued.

In this type of construction work, from two and one-half to three years are necessary to become marginally competent with tools. Then the real study begins—layout, complex geometry, organization, design—all while learning to maintain high standards and work quickly. In three years an apprentice may think he knows what he's doing, but he really doesn't.

For the first two or three years, an apprentice is essentially a dead weight, an economic liability to the teacher. Not only are apprentices paid at East Wind, but skilled and highly paid people, capable of quickly doing a large volume of high-quality work, have to teach them, show them what's dangerous, correct them, and try to salvage the very expensive lumber they may have ruined, which of course also represents a loss for the company. So why would anyone take on an apprentice? Perhaps because the teacher, like Brackett, feels his own skill entails a responsibility to pass it on. Some teachers also hope that the newly skilled apprentice will feel an obligation to his mentors and be willing to work for a few years at reduced wages to help defray the cost he represented to the company.

Brackett can predict from the very beginning how well apprentices will do by observing them performing menial tasks and watching how they do everything, including how they walk and their general level of attention. A skilled craftsman acts in a certain way that is evident to other craftsmen, even those in a different field. Brackett believes that people tend to show a consistent level of care and attention in every task. Generally if they do one job well, then they will do other jobs well. Patience and attention to detail can't be switched on and off like a light.

Brackett learned that the best way to teach is to give people the opportunity to make a mistake. Apprentices don't learn unless they have a chance to make a muck of it. According to him, stories of apprentices sweeping the shop floor for years and absorbing a craft are apocryphal. "Unless apprentices are given a chance to do worthwhile work and are challenged, they lose interest, as is only human. In Japan, they die spiritually, while in the United States they leave—and rightly so. When the inevitable mistake is made, however, then it is imperative that teacher and apprentice find out what went wrong and learn from it. To not do so and to make the same error again is cause for disappointment, as it should be, and results in unpleasantness in the shop or on site.

"In one house where I stayed in Kyoto," Brackett continued, "a remarkable woman lived upstairs. Nakamura Yaeko had left home and family to follow the spiritual path of tea ceremony just after the end of World War II. She taught the tea ceremony to Kyoto aristocracy and Zen students. At one point I knew that one of her principal students was also a craftsman, and I asked how his study of tea was going. She told me he was very skillful and had learned a lot in a short time. I told her I thought that sounded like a good thing, and she shook her head and said, 'No, that's not good, not good at all. To be really good he should make mistakes; he should learn how to do tea ceremony all wrong. Otherwise, his knowledge will be shallow, and he will think he knows more than he does. He will only know the right way to do this. It would be so much better if he also knew the wrong way.'

"I asked Nakamura-san on another occasion how I could be a good carpenter. She was one of the first female university graduates in Japan in an age when women didn't normally pursue higher education. For a while she had served as an interpreter for the Foreign Ministry and she had a great breadth of knowledge. She told me, 'You have to study *everything, everything.* You should know music and art and philosophy and chemistry, you should always study, since only then will you be able to use what you know of carpentry. Otherwise, you can only be good at one thing, and what you must learn is how to be human!'"

Brackett has softened the sometimes harsh Japanese master-apprentice relationship and has an affectionate, if sometimes tempestuous, bond with his staff, attempting to encourage good work with positive reinforcement. He says he tries not to lose his temper when mistakes are made, but he remains demanding to keep them on their toes. He wants them to be a little nervous around him in order to achieve the energy and tension that produce quality work. Unlike masters in Japan, he will overtly teach. "Americans expect that, and it's in my interest, since I am paying apprentices a lot more than I was paid in Japan. I want my men to hurry up and become skillful." He never allows someone to work for free: "Since unpaid people are free to go, their involvement is tenuous at best." Without payment, the seriousness of what both teacher and apprentice are doing is diluted, since the apprentice has to support himself with other work and cannot devote his full time and energy to learning. To Brackett, part-time apprenticeship is an oxymoron.

"Japanese carpentry can only be studied, never mastered," he asserts. "I think there are only about ten master carpenters in Japan today." He absolutely resists being labeled a master carpenter himself, insisting that he's a carpenter, that's all. In the context of where he learned his craft, his humility is appropriate.

"Certainly, the austerity of Zen Buddhism has had a significant influence upon Japanese architecture and craft, but not greater than Buddhism in general and what it says about work and how to live. Japanese temple carpenters are not disciples of Zen Buddhism, or usually of any school of Buddhism, but just as being Italian presumes an inextricable connection to Catholicism and its cultural influence, so being Japanese is to be influenced by Zen and Buddhism. These carpenters do their work with the single-mindedness of monks.

"Additionally, Shinto, the primeval animistic belief that all things are living, is part of the heart of traditional Japan, although this way of relating to the world is disappearing. Wood lives, tools live and have a spirit, and so do tea bowls and waterfalls and forest glades and buildings and kilns and silk. Traditionally the Japanese treated things with the respect one treats any life, which in many ways demonstrates an advanced culture very much in tune with nature. Temple carpenters are usually influenced by these sensibilities, particularly when it comes to wood and tools."

Brackett has come to believe that "teaching is really more important than the architecture itself. Without teaching there would be nothing but pitiful attempts at being 'artistic,' at being 'creative.' Just as the stone masons at Chartres built on centuries of shared knowledge, so too Japanese architecture can only be done well by the cognoscenti, by those who have received the tradition that went before to prepare their own seedbed of skill."

And yet he finds his philosophy is in contradiction to Western culture's definition of art, where a work is labeled art only if it is innovative or clever. "Artists and architects rarely seem to acknowledge those who came before them. Yet, they are but part of a continuum, inextricably indebted to their predecessors." Brackett views himself as a craftsman, a new, continually learning, Western link in a very old and continuous chain. He was taught, it was a great gift, and he must pass it on.

APPENDIX

Architectural Drawings

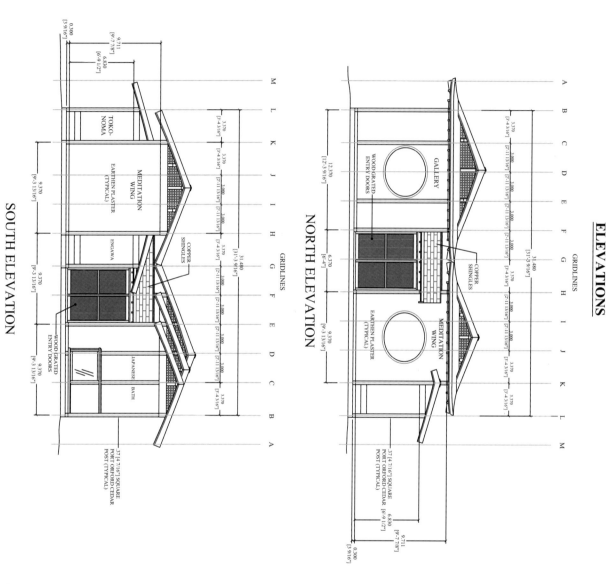

ELEVATIONS

GRIDLINES

NORTH ELEVATION

SOUTH ELEVATION

GRIDLINES

ELEVATIONS

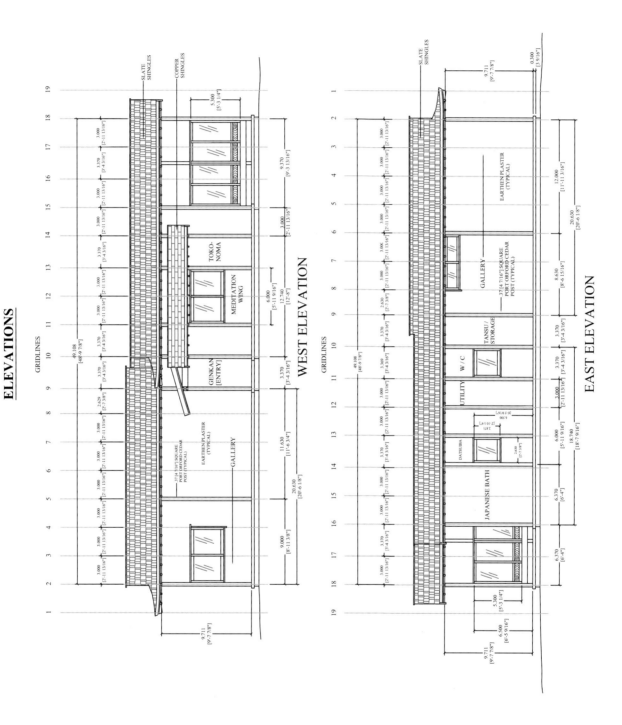

WEST ELEVATION

EAST ELEVATION

CEILING DETAILS
SECTIONS

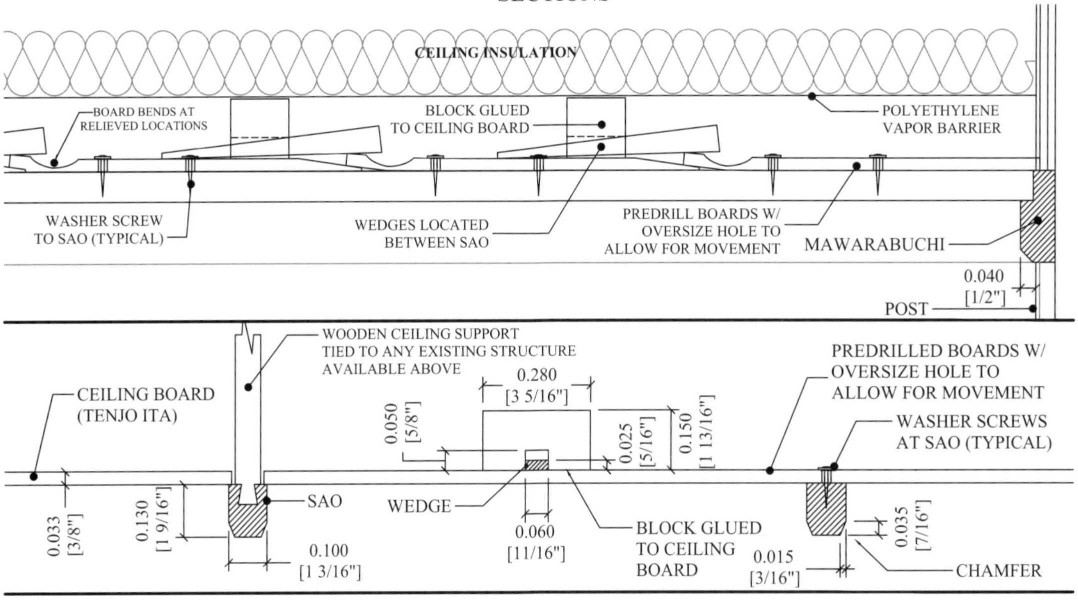

CEILING INSULATION

BOARD BENDS AT RELIEVED LOCATIONS

BLOCK GLUED TO CEILING BOARD

POLYETHYLENE VAPOR BARRIER

WASHER SCREW TO SAO (TYPICAL)

WEDGES LOCATED BETWEEN SAO

PREDRILL BOARDS W/ OVERSIZE HOLE TO ALLOW FOR MOVEMENT

MAWARABUCHI

0.040 [1/2"]

POST

WOODEN CEILING SUPPORT TIED TO ANY EXISTING STRUCTURE AVAILABLE ABOVE

CEILING BOARD (TENJO ITA)

PREDRILLED BOARDS W/ OVERSIZE HOLE TO ALLOW FOR MOVEMENT

WASHER SCREWS AT SAO (TYPICAL)

0.280 [3 5/16"]

0.050 [5/8"]

0.025 [5/16"]

0.150 [1 13/16"]

0.033 [3/8"]

0.130 [1 9/16"]

SAO

WEDGE

0.060 [11/16"]

BLOCK GLUED TO CEILING BOARD

0.015 [3/16"]

0.035 [7/16"]

CHAMFER

0.100 [1 3/16"]

PLAN

BLOCKS W/ WEDGES

WOODEN CEILING SUPPORT TIED TO ANY ROOF STRUCTURE AVAILABLE ABOVE

SAO SPACED AT OR NEAR 1.5 (17.89")

CEILING BOARDS

MAWARABUCHI

POST

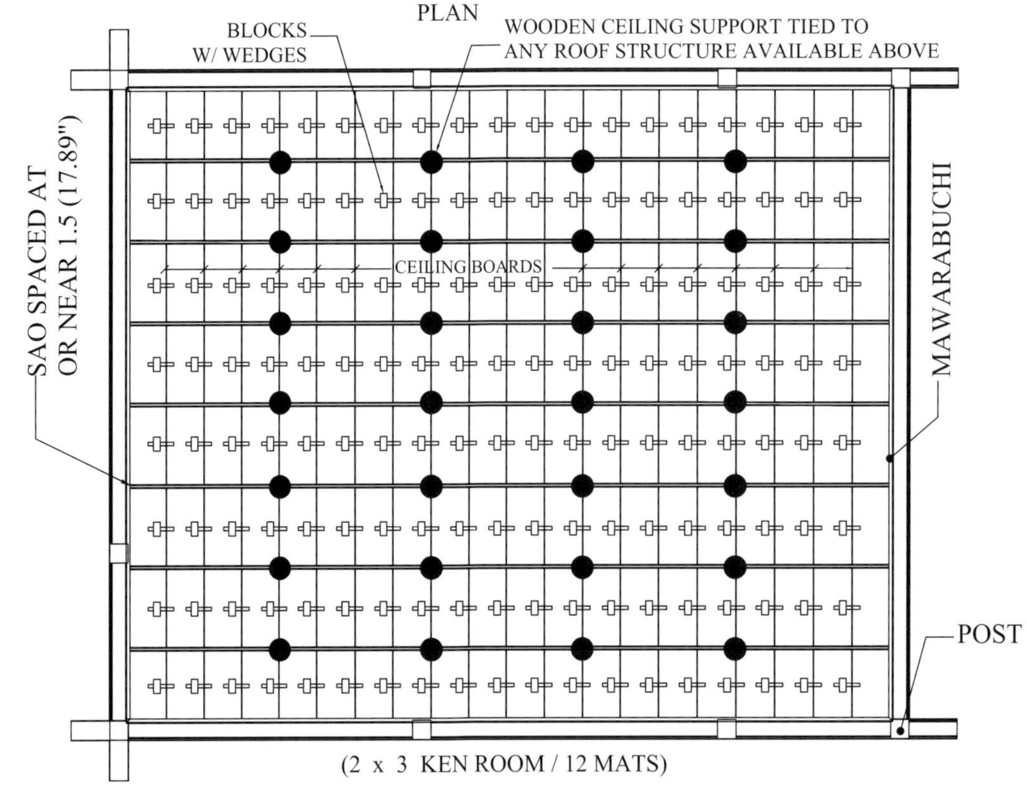

(2 x 3 KEN ROOM / 12 MATS)

GUEST HOUSE / ART GALLERY FLOOR PLAN

DECIMAL DIMENSIONS ARE SHAKU (JAPANESE DECIMAL FOOT)
[FEET AND INCHES IN BRACKETS]

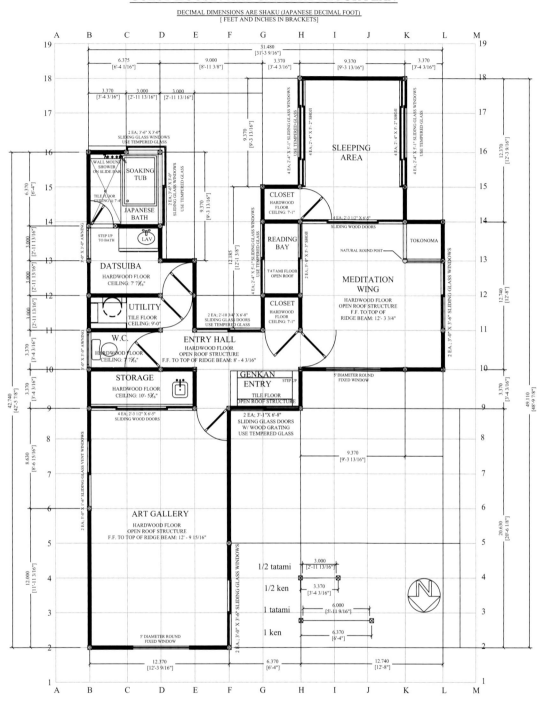

193

EAST WIND SHOIN (BAY WINDOW STUDY DESK)

INTERIOR ELEVATION

- CEILING BEYOND
- ROUND WINDOW
- BAMBOO, CAT TAIL STEMS, OR TREE BRANCHES TIED W/ WISTERIA VINES.

5.000
[4'-11 5/8"]

3.670
[3'-7 13/16"]

1.510
[1'-6"]

WOOD SLIDING DOORS

(1 KEN)

6.80
[6'-7 3/4"]

SECTION

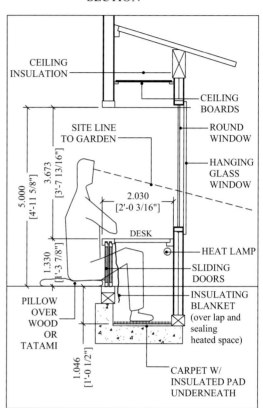

CEILING INSULATION

SITE LINE TO GARDEN

CEILING BOARDS

ROUND WINDOW

HANGING GLASS WINDOW

2.030
[2'-0 3/16"]

DESK

HEAT LAMP

SLIDING DOORS

INSULATING BLANKET (over lap and sealing heated space)

5.000
[4'-11 5/8"]

3.673
[3'-7 13/16"]

1.330
[1'-3 7/8"]

PILLOW OVER WOOD OR TATAMI

1.046
[1'-0 1/2"]

CARPET W/ INSULATED PAD UNDERNEATH

PLAN VIEW

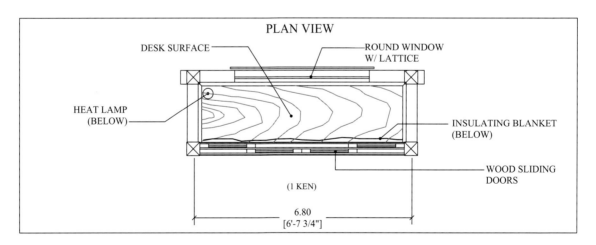

DESK SURFACE

ROUND WINDOW W/ LATTICE

HEAT LAMP (BELOW)

INSULATING BLANKET (BELOW)

WOOD SLIDING DOORS

(1 KEN)

6.80
[6'-7 3/4"]

KENSAO KETA YUKI (KETA WAY)

SIDE VIEW

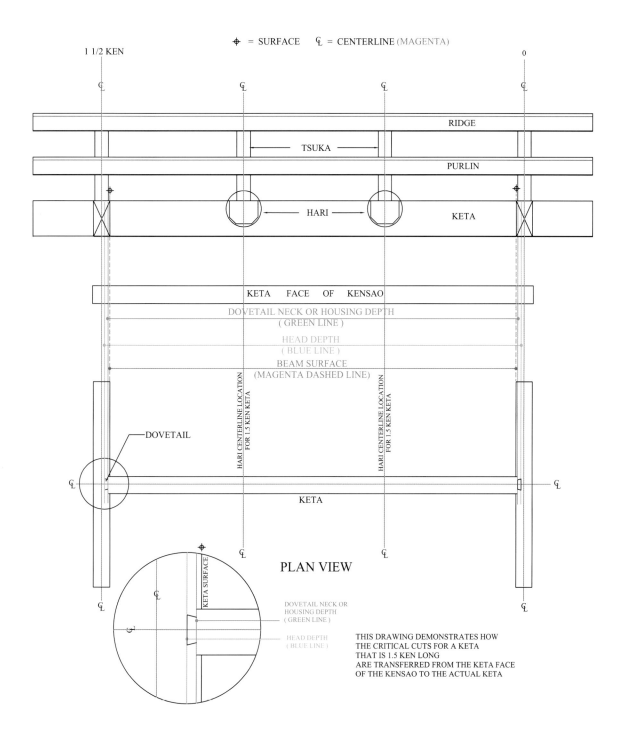

⊕ = SURFACE   ₵ = CENTERLINE (MAGENTA)

1 1/2 KEN

0

RIDGE

TSUKA

PURLIN

HARI

KETA

KETA   FACE   OF   KENSAO

DOVETAIL NECK OR HOUSING DEPTH
(GREEN LINE)

HEAD DEPTH
(BLUE LINE)

BEAM SURFACE
(MAGENTA DASHED LINE)

HARI CENTERLINE LOCATION
FOR 1.5 KEN KETA

HARI CENTERLINE LOCATION
FOR 1.5 KEN KETA

DOVETAIL

KETA

KETA SURFACE

PLAN VIEW

DOVETAIL NECK OR
HOUSING DEPTH
(GREEN LINE)

HEAD DEPTH
(BLUE LINE)

THIS DRAWING DEMONSTRATES HOW
THE CRITICAL CUTS FOR A KETA
THAT IS 1.5 KEN LONG
ARE TRANSFERRED FROM THE KETA FACE
OF THE KENSAO TO THE ACTUAL KETA

THE KENSAO

POST = .36 / TATAMI (KYOTO) = 3.15 X 6.30

1 KEN = 1/2 POST + 1 TATAMI + 1/2 POST (.18 + 6.30 + .18) = 6.66

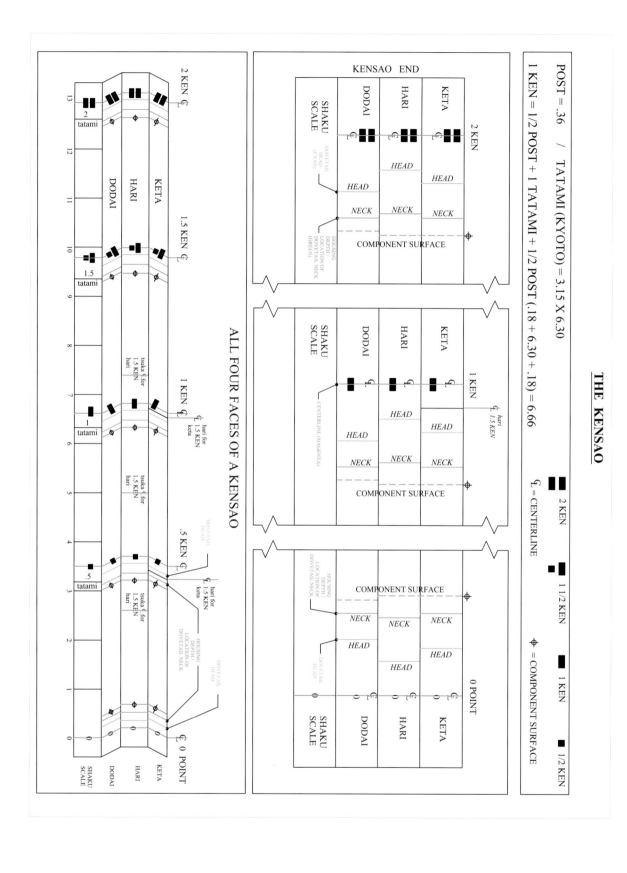

ALL FOUR FACES OF A KENSAO

KENSAO HARI YUKI (HARI WAY)

SIDE VIEW

1 1/2 KEN   ⊕ = SURFACE   ₵ = CENTERLINE (MAGENTA)

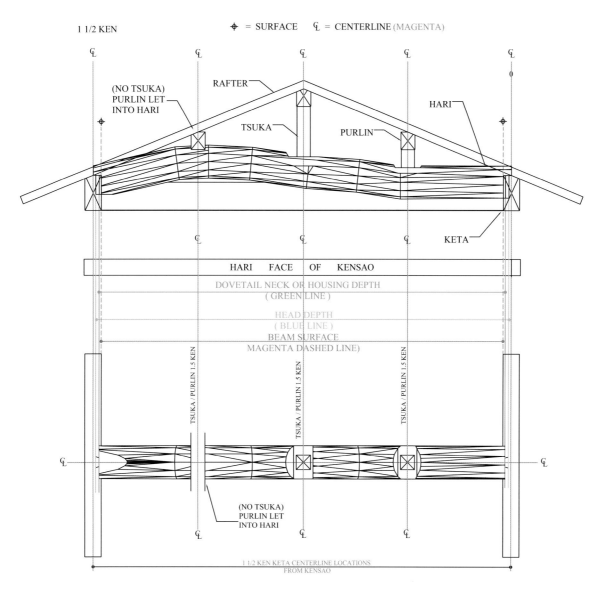

(NO TSUKA)
PURLIN LET
INTO HARI

RAFTER

TSUKA

PURLIN

HARI

KETA

HARI   FACE   OF   KENSAO

DOVETAIL NECK OR HOUSING DEPTH
(GREEN LINE)

HEAD DEPTH
(BLUE LINE)
BEAM SURFACE
MAGENTA DASHED LINE)

TSUKA / PURLIN 1.5 KEN

(NO TSUKA)
PURLIN LET
INTO HARI

1 1/2 KEN KETA CENTERLINE LOCATIONS
FROM KENSAO

PLAN VIEW

THIS DRAWING DEMONSTRATES HOW THE CRITICAL
CUTS FOR A HARI THAT IS 1.5 KEN LONG ARE TRANSFERRED
FROM THE HARI FACE OF THE KENSAO TO THE HARI.

TYPICAL INSULATED WALL W/ JAPANESE PLASTER SYSTEM

INTERIOR   EXTERIOR

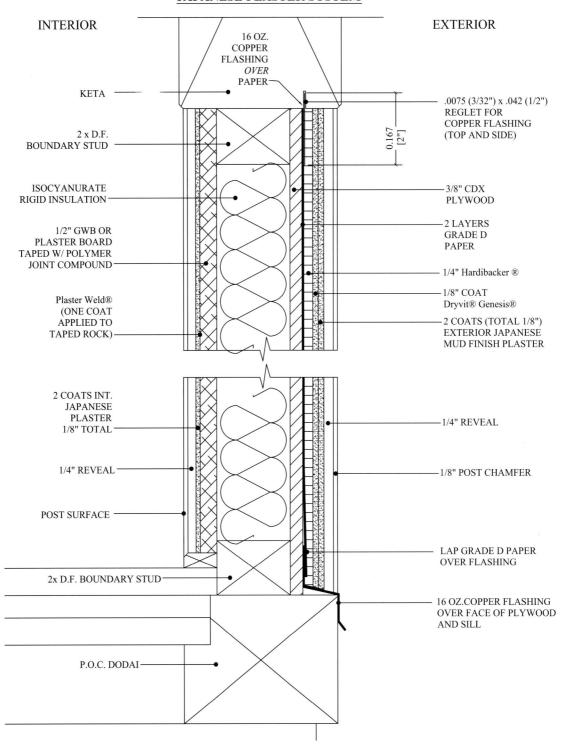

16 OZ. COPPER FLASHING *OVER* PAPER

KETA

2 x D.F. BOUNDARY STUD

ISOCYANURATE RIGID INSULATION

1/2" GWB OR PLASTER BOARD TAPED W/ POLYMER JOINT COMPOUND

Plaster Weld® (ONE COAT APPLIED TO TAPED ROCK)

2 COATS INT. JAPANESE PLASTER 1/8" TOTAL

1/4" REVEAL

POST SURFACE

2x D.F. BOUNDARY STUD

P.O.C. DODAI

.0075 (3/32") x .042 (1/2") REGLET FOR COPPER FLASHING (TOP AND SIDE)

0.167 [2"]

3/8" CDX PLYWOOD

2 LAYERS GRADE D PAPER

1/4" Hardibacker ®

1/8" COAT Dryvit® Genesis®

2 COATS (TOTAL 1/8") EXTERIOR JAPANESE MUD FINISH PLASTER

1/4" REVEAL

1/8" POST CHAMFER

LAP GRADE D PAPER OVER FLASHING

16 OZ.COPPER FLASHING OVER FACE OF PLYWOOD AND SILL

EXTERIOR WALL FLASHINGS

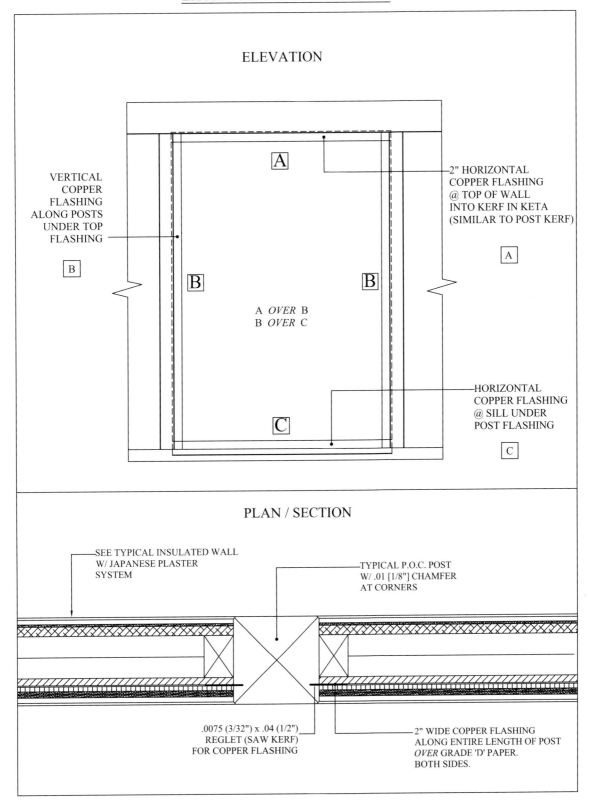

ELEVATION

Ⓐ

VERTICAL COPPER FLASHING ALONG POSTS UNDER TOP FLASHING

2" HORIZONTAL COPPER FLASHING @ TOP OF WALL INTO KERF IN KETA (SIMILAR TO POST KERF)

Ⓐ

Ⓑ   Ⓑ   Ⓑ

A *OVER* B
B *OVER* C

HORIZONTAL COPPER FLASHING @ SILL UNDER POST FLASHING

Ⓒ

Ⓒ

PLAN / SECTION

SEE TYPICAL INSULATED WALL W/ JAPANESE PLASTER SYSTEM

TYPICAL P.O.C. POST W/ .01 [1/8"] CHAMFER AT CORNERS

.0075 (3/32") x .04 (1/2") REGLET (SAW KERF) FOR COPPER FLASHING

2" WIDE COPPER FLASHING ALONG ENTIRE LENGTH OF POST *OVER* GRADE 'D' PAPER. BOTH SIDES.

199

UNINSULATED ROOF EAVE DETAILS

3/8" FINISH ROOF BOARDS
AT EAVES ONLY

FINISH RAFTER
W/ .01 (1/8")
CHAMFER

BEVEL CUT PREVENTS
SAGGING BETWEEN RAFTERS

FINISH ROOFING
MATERIAL

UNDERLAYMENT

3/4" OR 5/8"
CDX PLYWOOD

0.03
[3/8"]

0.06
[3/4"]

0.09
[1 1/8"]

0.04
[1/2"]

0.04
[1/2"]

80 - 100%
POST DIMENSION

0.05
[5/8"]

.01 (1/8")
CHAMFER

COPPER FLASHING
W/ COPPER NAIL

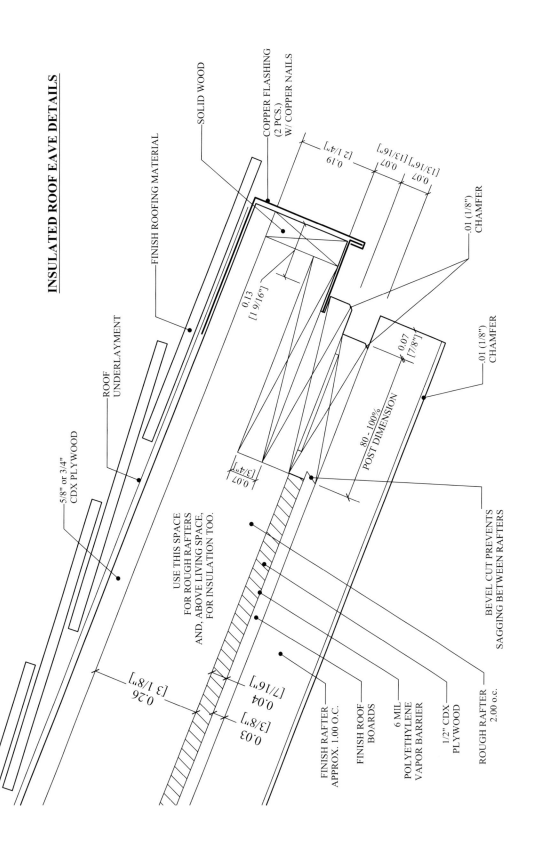

INSULATED ROOF EAVE DETAILS

FINISH ROOFING MATERIAL

SOLID WOOD

COPPER FLASHING (2 PCS.) W/ COPPER NAILS

ROOF UNDERLAYMENT

5/8" or 3/4" CDX PLYWOOD

0.19 [2 1/4"]

0.07 [13/16"] 0.07 [13/16"]

.01 (1/8") CHAMFER

0.13 [1 9/16"]

0.07 [3/4"]

0.07 [7/8"]

.01 (1/8") CHAMFER

POST DIMENSION 80 - 100%

USE THIS SPACE FOR ROUGH RAFTERS AND, ABOVE LIVING SPACE, FOR INSULATION TOO.

0.26 [3 1/8"]

0.04 [7/16"]

0.03 [3/8"]

FINISH RAFTER APPROX. 1.00 O.C.

FINISH ROOF BOARDS

6 MIL POLYETHYLENE VAPOR BARRIER

1/2" CDX PLYWOOD

ROUGH RAFTER 2.00 o.c.

BEVEL CUT PREVENTS SAGGING BETWEEN RAFTERS

ROOF EAVES

201

SLIDING GLASS DOOR DETAILS

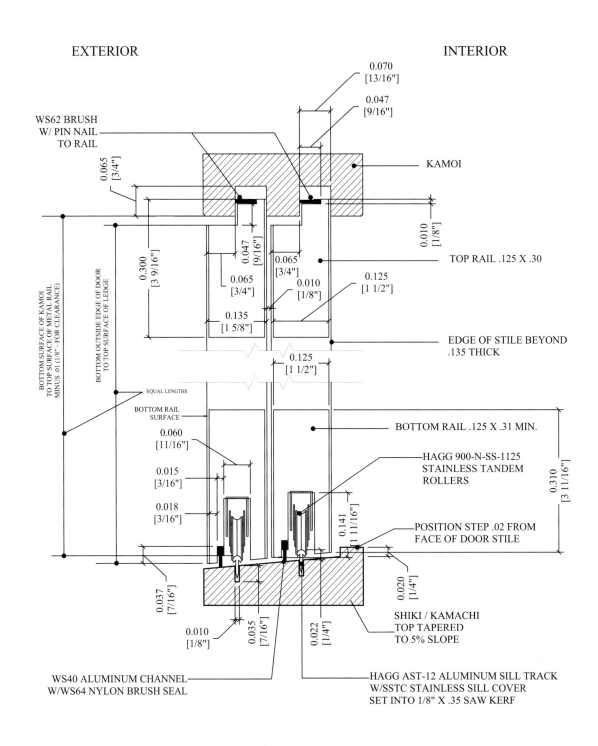

EXTERIOR

INTERIOR

0.070
[13/16"]

0.047
[9/16"]

WS62 BRUSH
W/ PIN NAIL
TO RAIL

KAMOI

0.065
[3/4"]

0.010
[1/8"]

0.047
[9/16"]

0.300
[3 9/16"]

0.065
[3/4"]

TOP RAIL .125 X .30

0.065
[3/4"]

0.010
[1/8"]

0.125
[1 1/2"]

0.135
[1 5/8"]

EDGE OF STILE BEYOND
.135 THICK

BOTTOM SURFACE OF KAMOI
TO TOP SURFACE OF METAL RAIL
MINUS .01 (1/8"- FOR CLEARANCE)

BOTTOM OUTSIDE EDGE OF DOOR
TO TOP SURFACE OF LEDGE

0.125
[1 1/2"]

EQUAL LENGTHS

BOTTOM RAIL
SURFACE

BOTTOM RAIL .125 X .31 MIN.

0.060
[11/16"]

HAGG 900-N-SS-1125
STAINLESS TANDEM
ROLLERS

0.015
[3/16"]

0.310
[3 11/16"]

0.018
[3/16"]

0.141
[1 11/16"]

POSITION STEP .02 FROM
FACE OF DOOR STILE

0.020
[1/4"]

0.037
[7/16"]

0.010
[1/8"]

0.035
[7/16"]

0.022
[1/4"]

SHIKI / KAMACHI
TOP TAPERED
TO 5% SLOPE

WS40 ALUMINUM CHANNEL
W/WS64 NYLON BRUSH SEAL

HAGG AST-12 ALUMINUM SILL TRACK
W/SSTC STAINLESS SILL COVER
SET INTO 1/8" X .35 SAW KERF

SLIDING GLASS DOOR WEATHERSTRIPPING

DETAILS

WS88 LEAFSEAL WITH SPLINE AND DADO. CUT 2mm x 8mm DADO IN STILE EDGE FOR LEAFSEAL INSERTION. THE DADO IN THE EDGE OF STILE SHOULD BE .02 [1/4"] WIDER THAN THE SPLINE INSTALLED IN POST TO ALLOW FOR AN AVERAGE .01[1/8"] CLEARANCE BETWEEN SPLINE AND EDGE OF DADO.

ALL WEATHER STRIPPING AVAILABLE FROM RESOURCE CONSERVATION TECHNOLOGY INC.

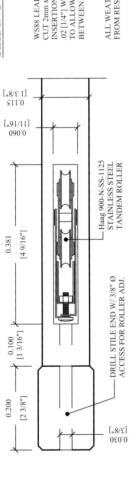

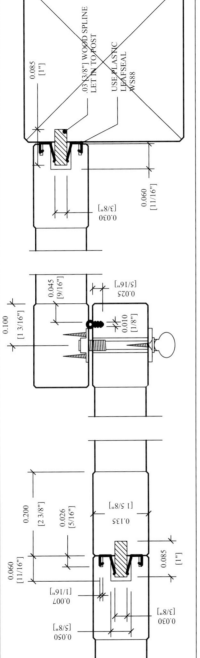

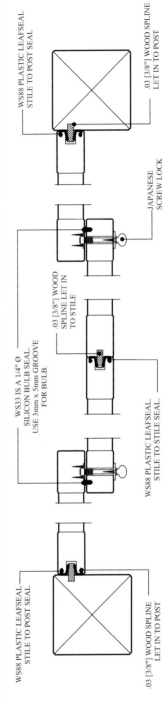

TYPICAL JAPANESE BATH

SECTION

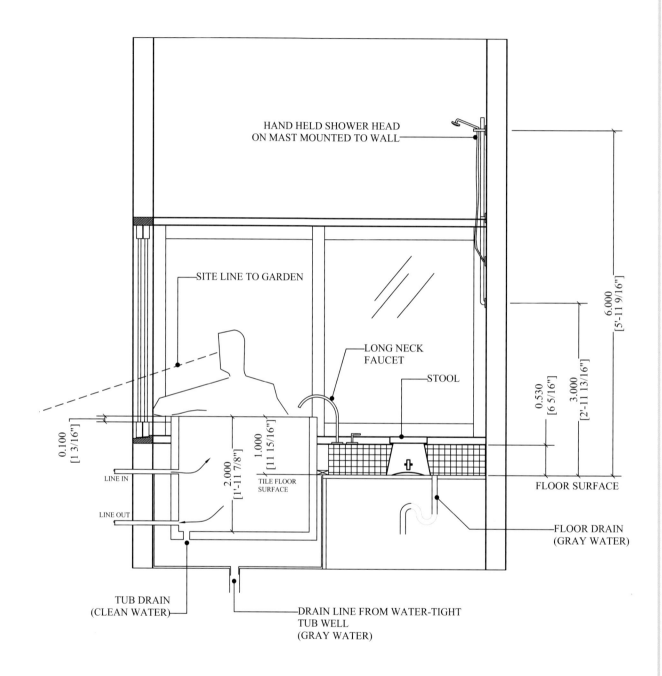

HAND HELD SHOWER HEAD
ON MAST MOUNTED TO WALL

SITE LINE TO GARDEN

LONG NECK
FAUCET

STOOL

6.000
[5'-11 9/16"]

0.530
[6 5/16"]

3.000
[2'-11 13/16"]

0.100
[1 3/16"]

LINE IN

LINE OUT

2.000
[1'-11 7/8"]

1.000
[11 15/16"]

TILE FLOOR
SURFACE

FLOOR SURFACE

FLOOR DRAIN
(GRAY WATER)

TUB DRAIN
(CLEAN WATER)

DRAIN LINE FROM WATER-TIGHT
TUB WELL
(GRAY WATER)

TYPICAL JAPANESE BATH

FLOOR PLAN

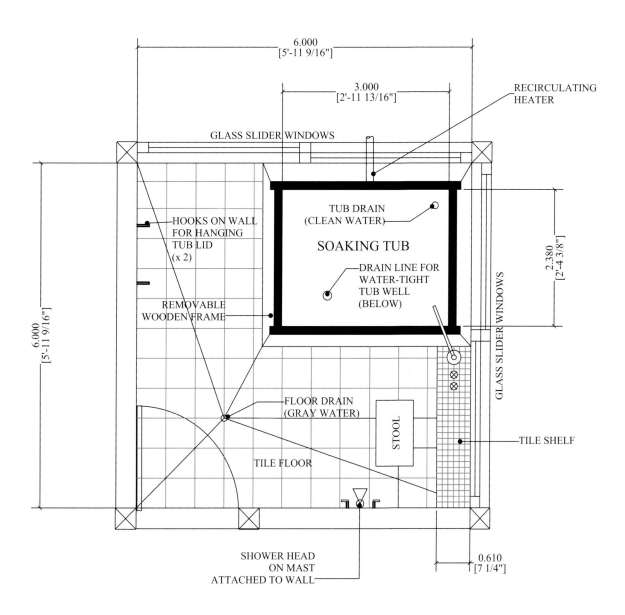

6.000
[5'-11 9/16"]

3.000
[2'-11 13/16"]

RECIRCULATING
HEATER

GLASS SLIDER WINDOWS

TUB DRAIN
(CLEAN WATER)

HOOKS ON WALL
FOR HANGING
TUB LID
(x 2)

SOAKING TUB

DRAIN LINE FOR
WATER-TIGHT
TUB WELL
(BELOW)

2.380
[2'-4 3/8"]

REMOVABLE
WOODEN FRAME

GLASS SLIDER WINDOWS

6.000
[5'-11 9/16"]

FLOOR DRAIN
(GRAY WATER)

STOOL

TILE SHELF

TILE FLOOR

0.610
[7 1/4"]

SHOWER HEAD
ON MAST
ATTACHED TO WALL

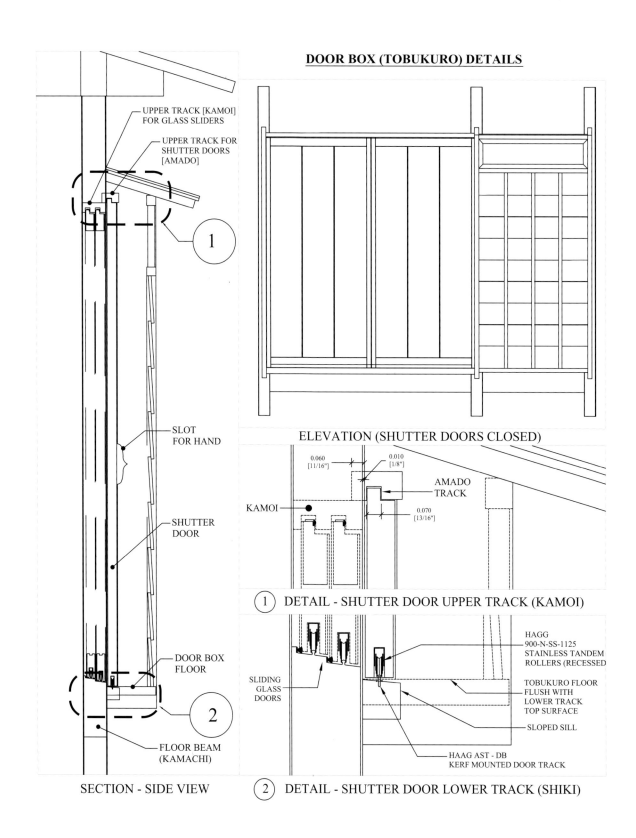

DOOR BOX (TOBUKURO) DETAILS

UPPER TRACK [KAMOI] FOR GLASS SLIDERS

UPPER TRACK FOR SHUTTER DOORS [AMADO]

①

SLOT FOR HAND

SHUTTER DOOR

DOOR BOX FLOOR

②

FLOOR BEAM (KAMACHI)

SECTION - SIDE VIEW

ELEVATION (SHUTTER DOORS CLOSED)

0.060 [11/16"]

0.010 [1/8"]

AMADO TRACK

KAMOI

0.070 [13/16"]

① **DETAIL - SHUTTER DOOR UPPER TRACK (KAMOI)**

HAGG 900-N-SS-1125 STAINLESS TANDEM ROLLERS (RECESSED

SLIDING GLASS DOORS

TOBUKURO FLOOR FLUSH WITH LOWER TRACK TOP SURFACE

SLOPED SILL

HAAG AST - DB KERF MOUNTED DOOR TRACK

② **DETAIL - SHUTTER DOOR LOWER TRACK (SHIKI)**

AMADO

SHUTTER DOORS, SCREENS (AMADO) AND DOOR BOX (TOBUKURO)

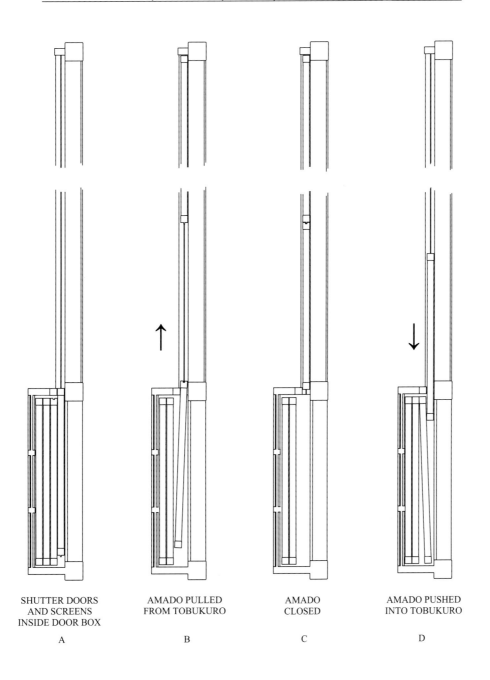

SHUTTER DOORS AND SCREENS INSIDE DOOR BOX	AMADO PULLED FROM TOBUKURO	AMADO CLOSED	AMADO PUSHED INTO TOBUKURO
A	B	C	D

STAGES OF OPERATION

FLOOR HEATING REGISTER DETAILS

PLAN

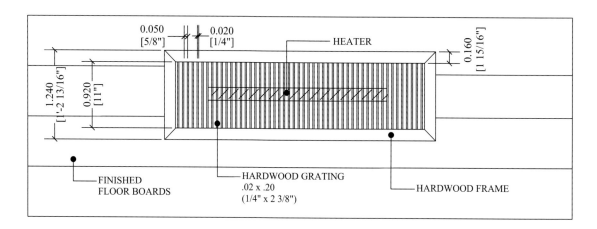

0.050 [5/8"] 0.020 [1/4"] HEATER 0.160 [1 15/16"]

1.240 [1'-2 13/16"] 0.920 [11"]

FINISHED FLOOR BOARDS

HARDWOOD GRATING .02 x .20 (1/4" x 2 3/8")

HARDWOOD FRAME

SECTIONS

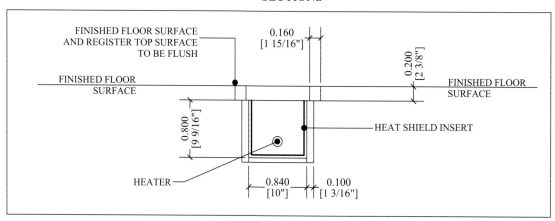

FINISHED FLOOR SURFACE AND REGISTER TOP SURFACE TO BE FLUSH

0.160 [1 15/16"] 0.200 [2 3/8"]

FINISHED FLOOR SURFACE FINISHED FLOOR SURFACE

0.800 [9 9/16"]

HEAT SHIELD INSERT

HEATER

0.840 [10"] 0.100 [1 3/16"]

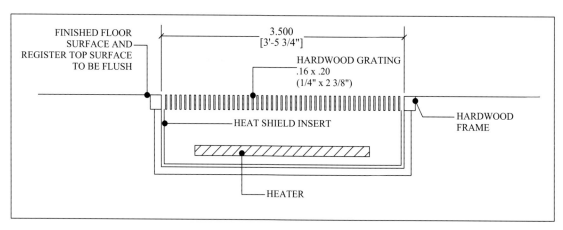

FINISHED FLOOR SURFACE AND REGISTER TOP SURFACE TO BE FLUSH

3.500 [3'-5 3/4"]

HARDWOOD GRATING .16 x .20 (1/4" x 2 3/8")

HEAT SHIELD INSERT

HARDWOOD FRAME

HEATER

EAST WIND RAISED ENGAWA

SECTION

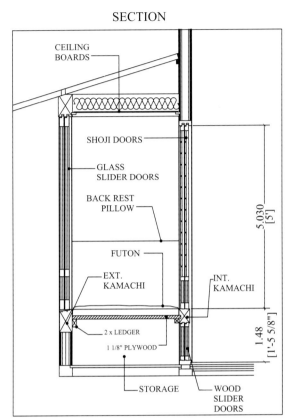

CEILING BOARDS

SHOJI DOORS

GLASS SLIDER DOORS

BACK REST PILLOW

FUTON

EXT. KAMACHI

INT. KAMACHI

2 x LEDGER

1 1/8" PLYWOOD

5.030 [5']

1.48 [1'-5 5/8"]

STORAGE

WOOD SLIDER DOORS

ELEVATION

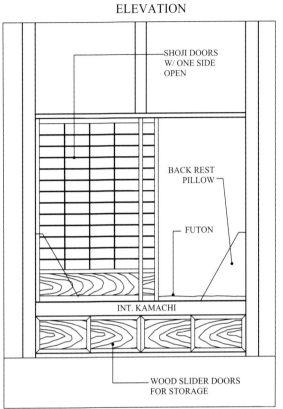

SHOJI DOORS W/ ONE SIDE OPEN

BACK REST PILLOW

FUTON

INT. KAMACHI

WOOD SLIDER DOORS FOR STORAGE

PLAN

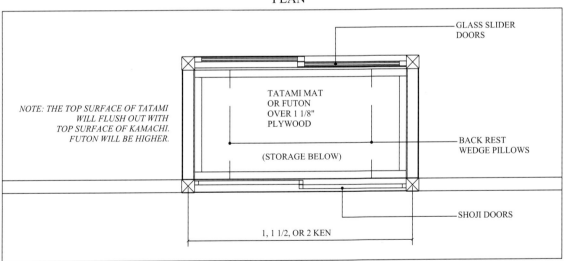

GLASS SLIDER DOORS

NOTE: THE TOP SURFACE OF TATAMI WILL FLUSH OUT WITH TOP SURFACE OF KAMACHI. FUTON WILL BE HIGHER.

TATAMI MAT OR FUTON OVER 1 1/8" PLYWOOD

(STORAGE BELOW)

BACK REST WEDGE PILLOWS

SHOJI DOORS

1, 1 1/2, OR 2 KEN

Glossary

ajiro. Basket weave of very thin strips of wood, a technique used occasionally for ceilings and less frequently for door panels.

amado. Interlocking wooden doors that shutter an open expanse between posts.

awaseido. Final finish whetstone.

board foot. Measure of lumber volume: a piece of wood 1 inch thick, 12 inches wide, and 1 foot long.

bu. Unit of measure for 0.1 *sun*, approximately 3.03 millimeters.

chamfer. Bevel.

checking. Cracking in wood.

datsuiba. Dressing area next to Japanese tub.

dodai. Horizontal timber or ground sill under the posts that supports the posts and frequently the floor structure.

engawa. Veranda or hallway located on exterior walls that can be opened to the outside.

engawa hashira. Veranda post.

equilibrium moisture content. Point where wood's moisture content is in equilibrium with the atmospheric relative humidity, neither accepting nor losing moisture. Such wood is regarded as "dry."

flat-sawn. Sawn at a right angle to radius of log. Also called plain-sawn, flat grain, or tangential grain.

fusuma. Wooden sliding panels covered with opaque paper or fabric.

futon. Folding Japanese bedding used on tatami, and stored away when not in use.

genkan. Entry hall.

gensun. Full-scale layout of house drawn on plywood.

goza. Upper surface of a tatami mat made of woven reeds.

hafu. Barge rafters, wide boards at gable ends that give roof its shape.

hari. Log beams.

hashira. Post.

heri. Silk border edging a tatami.

hikite. Finger pull, usually set into a door.

hipped roof. Distinctive shape created by placing large rafters on a diagonal from a corner to the ridge.

hirogomae. Eaves board installed wide face flat on top of rafters.

hold down. Special hardware for bolting a structural member to the underlying foundation.

honbashira. Principal post.

hondaruki. Main roof rafters.

irimoya. Hipped gable roof, a Dutch gable.

ita-zu. Floor plan of basic layouts drawn on board with grid locating components, traditionally the only plan needed to build.

kamachi. Floor-level horizontal timber that supports floors or walls between the posts. It is supported by the posts, to which it is joined.

kama tsugi. Type of scarf joint.

kamoi. Door and window head.

kanawa tsugi. Type of scarf joint.

kanban ita. Plan board (see ita-zu).

ken. Standard building module, equal to a tatami's length (approximately 6 feet) plus half the width of the standard posts at each end. This is always a post center-to-center dimension.

kensao. Measuring stick used for layout.

kento tsuka. Short supporting post below a sill or beam.

kerf. Very thin groove, the cut of a saw blade.

keta. Perimeter or transverse beam.

kiwari. Traditional system of determining the size of all the building's components based on a proportion of principal posts.

kokabe. Wall surface between door heads and ceiling.

koku Measure of lumber volume, a piece of wood 1 *shaku* (1 foot) thick by 1 *shaku* (1 foot) wide by 10 *shaku* long.

koshi ita. Base panel of a door or shoji.

kumiko. Grid of a shoji to which paper is applied.

kutsubako. Shoe cabinet.

mawaribuchi. Ceiling molding.

mendo ita. Literally "trouble board." This eaves blocking is inserted in the space between perimeter beams and finish roof and between rafters to block that space.

minka. Folk house, usually denoting a country farmhouse, but applicable to urban folk houses.

mo. Japanese unit of measure for one-tenth of a *rin*, approximately 0.0303 millimeters.

mortise. Hole cut in lumber to receive a tenon.

moya. Purlins.

mune. Ridge.

nageshi. Trim piece above heads.

nori. Glue.

nuki. Largest structural member found within traditional mud wall. In some (especially ceremonial) buildings, the *nuki* will be oversized and employed as a visual element.

obiki. Girders to support large floor spans.

osamari. Unified, effortless integration of the detailing of the house.

oshiire. Closet, usually about three feet deep and running along a room.

otoshigake. Extra thick head in a *tokonoma* opening.

pecky. Dry rot infestation in some lumbers, usually cedars and redwoods.

purlin. Roof timber running the length of roof, parallel to the ridge and similar to it.

quarter-sawn. Milling method that produces lumber that is neither vertical grain nor flat grain, but has qualities of both.

ranma. Decorative wood panel that fills gap between ceiling and door or window heads, i.e., a transom.

ranma kamoi. Transom head.

ranma shiki. Lower track for transom.

rin. Japanese unit of measure for one-tenth of a *bu*, approximately 0.303 millimeters.

sao. Ceiling stringer.

sashigane. Carpenter's square, one of three sacred tools.

seiwari. Lengthwise cut made to the center of a log to prevent random checking as it dries.

shaku. Japanese unit of measure that is 11.930406 inches, almost a foot, or 30.3 centimeters.

shatchi. Spline inserted in a joint to cinch it tight.

shear wall. Rigid wall between posts designed to resist lateral loads.

shiki. Lower tracks for sliding doors or windows.

shin ita. Finished board at edge of thick eaves, common in temple architecture, used in contemporary residential architecture to enclose a thick structure containing roof insulation.

shitaji. Smallest of bamboo lattices within plaster walls.

soffit. "Box" constructed to conceal or protect an architectural feature, such as a beam or a cornice.

sudare. Hanging mat made of rushes or bamboo to screen sunlight from a house or to provide privacy. Usually hung from the eaves.

sukiya. Teahouse-style architecture.

sumigi. Hip rafter.

sumisashi. Pen made of split bamboo, one of three sacred tools.

sumitsubo. Inkpot with inkline, one of three sacred tools.

sun. Unit of measure for one-tenth of a *shaku*, approximately 3.03 centimeters.

tanigi. Valley rafter, similar to sumigi.

tansu. Storage chest.

taruki. Rafter.

tarukigake. Ledger board on which lean-to rafters rest.

tatami. Floor covering mat made of woven reeds over core of rice straw, generally 3 x 6 feet in length and width and about 2^1/8 inches thick.

tenjo. Suspended ceiling.

tenon. Extension of a member that is inserted into a hole cut for it called a mortise.

toko. Inner rice straw core of tatami.

tokonoma. Display alcove found in traditional Japanese architecture.

toryo. Head carpenter in charge of shop and construction site.

tsuka. Short posts that support roof structures like

purlins and ridges, i.e., queen posts.

tsukegamoi. Extension of door and window heads applied to walls all around room forming a continuous line.

tsunagi. Tie beams.

tsuri tsuka. Hanging posts that support members below them like door or window heads or even structural members.

ura ita. Finished roof board, visible from within.

vertical-sawn. Cut along the radius, also called radially-sawn.

washi. Translucent handmade paper, most often made from inner bark of branches of mulberry bush.

yagiri. Decorative gable grating or grid.

yodoya. Roof eaves component resting directly on eaves fascia.

yukimi shoji. Snow-viewing shoji. Refers to panels in shoji that slide up to allow view through window of falling snow.

Resources

CHAPTER ONE

East Wind (Higashi Kaze) Inc.
21020 Shields Camp Road
Nevada City, CA 95959
Tel: (530) 265-3744
Fax: (530)265-6994
E-mail: mail@eastwindinc.com
www.eastwindinc.com

CHAPTER THREE

Lumber from well-managed, FSC-certified forests
The Collins Companies (Collins Pine)
1618 S. W. First Avenue, Ste. 500
Portland, OR 97201
Tel: 800-329-1219
Fax: 503-417-1441
E-mail: mluza@collinsco.com
www.CollinsWood.com

Veneer quality burls and logs
Quail Valley Veneer
Skyler Phelps
13960 Camino del Lego
Auburn, CA 95602
Tel: 530-269-2403

Radio frequency vacuum kiln drying of lumber
Fraserwood Industries
P.O. Box 175
Garibaldi Highlands
British Columbia
Canada VoN 1To
Tel: 604-892-7562
Fax: 604-898-1384
E-mail: info@www.fraserwoodindustries.com
www.fraserwoodindustries.com

CHAPTER FOUR

Custom-made carbide tooling, bits, saw blades
Crown Carbide Inc.
3540 42nd Avenue
Sacramento, CA 95824
Tel: 916-391-9700
Fax: 916-391-9176

Japanese carpenter tools, hardware, books, manuals and plastering supplies
Hida Tool & Hardware
1333 San Pablo Ave
Berkeley, CA 94702
Tel: 800-443-5512 or 510-524-3700

Fax: 510-524-3423

E-mail: hidatool.com@hidatool.com

www.hidatool.com

Japanese tools and hardware

Japan Woodworker Catalog

1731 Clement Avenue

Alameda, CA 94501

Tel: 800-537-7820 or 510-521-1810

E-mail: support@thejapanwoodworker.com

www.japanwoodworker.com

Japanese woodworking tools and building materials

HMS Enterprises, Inc.

51 Shattuck Street

Pepperell, MA 01463

Toll free 877-My Bench (692-3624)

Int. 1-978-433-6927

Fax: 978-433-4951

E-mail: hms@japanesetools.com

www.japanesetools.com

CHAPTER FIVE

Foundations and general building contractor

Morris G. Stoumen

5230 McFarlane Road

Sebastopol, CA 95472

Tel: 707-829-9180

Cell: 707-318-0733

E-mail: stoumen@pon.net

Structural engineering for Japanese timber frames

Tom Tormey Engineering Consultant

369-B Third Street, #364

San Rafael, CA 94901

Tel: 415-453-8420

Fax: 415-453-8368

ttormey@pacbell.net

Copper and slate roof work

C. F. Slating

P.O. Box 224

Fairfax, CA 94978

Tel: 415-451 4784

Fax: 415-485-0186

E-mail: cam112358@earthlink.net

www.cfslating.com

Non ferrous metals, nails, sheet, coils, fasteners, wire

R. J. Leahy

1475 Yosemite Avenue

San Francisco, CA 94124

Tel: 800-514-4106 or 415-861-7161

Fax: 415-822-2689

E-mail: sales@rjleahy.com

www.rjleahy.com

CHAPTER SIX

Energy and mechanical engineering

Melas Energy Engineering

547 Uren Street

Nevada City, CA 95959

Tel: 530-265-2492

Fax: 530-265-2273

E-mail: mmelas@sbcglobal.net

www.melas-energy.com

Japanese tubs, square & barrel, and hot tubs

Roberts Hot Tubs

2343 Welcome Avenue

Richmond, CA 94804

800-735-5290

Tel: 510-234-7920

E-mail: info@rhtubs.com

www.rhtubs.com

Plumbing fixtures

Plumbing N' Things
1620 Industrial Way
Redwood City, CA 94063
Tel: 650-363-7333
Fax: 650-367-6369
E-mail: tonib@plumbingnthings.com

Granite sinks

Stone Forest
Tel: 888-682-2987
Fax: 505-982-2712
E-mail: info@stoneforest.com
www.stoneforest.com

American and European door and window hardware

Baldwin Brass Center of CA, Inc.
2119 San Pablo Avenue
Berkeley, CA 94702
Tel: 510-548-5757
Fax: 510-548-4342
www.belmont hardware.com

Bronze-alloy awning window hinges and casement fasteners

C. Winslow Company
3501 Sunnyside Blvd.
Marysville, WA 98270
Tel: 425-334-1772
Fax: 425-335-0382
E-mail: cwinco1772@aol.com

Window/door glazing supplies, caulking and waterproofing materials

D. M. Figley Co Inc.
10 Kelly Court
Menlo Park, CA 94025
Tel: 650-329-8700 or 800-292-9919
Fax: 650-329-0601

E-mail: info@dmfigley.com
www.dmfigley.com

Door, window and skylight hardware

Functional Fenestration
12612 Crenshaw Boulevard
Hawthorne, CA 90250
Tel: 800-677-0228 or 323-756-9971
Fax: 323-242-3824
E-mail: sales@fenestration.net
www.fenestration.net

Weather stripping as seen in Appendix

Resource Conservation Technology Inc.
2233 Huntingdon Avenue
Baltimore, MD 21211
Tel: 410-366-1146
Fax: 410-366-1202
www.conservationtechnology.com

Electrical Work

California Solar Electric Co.
10141 Evening Star Drive, Suite 6
Grass Valley, California 95945
Tel: 530-274-3671
Fax: 530-274-7518
E-mail: contact@californiasolarco.com
www.californiasolarco.com

Custom doors and windows, architectural millwork, carvings

Sierra Woods Inc.
P.O. Box 1846
Nevada City, CA 95959
Tel: 530-265-5354
Fax: 530-265-4918
E-mail: design@sierrawoods.com
www.sierrawoods.com

Insulated glass products

Thermalsun
3250 Brickway Blvd. Suite B
Santa Rosa, CA 95403
Tel: 800-400-4786
Fax: 707-579-9939
E-mail: info@thermalsun.com
www.thermalsun.com

Glazing supplies

C.R. Laurence Co.
2503 East Vernon Avenue
Los Angeles, CA 90058
Tel: 800-421-6144
Fax: 800-262-3299
E-mail: cust_serv@crlaurance.com
www.crlaurance.com

Japanese tools, hardware, shoji paper, supplies

Misugi Designs
3276 Formby Lane
Fairfield, CA 94534
Tel: 707-422-0734
Fax: 707-425-2465
E-mail: misugidesigns@hotmail.com
www.misugidesigns.com

Tools, hardware, shoji paper and glue

Soko Hardware Company
Japan Town Center
1698 Post Street
San Francisco, CA 94115
Tel: 415-931-5510
Fax: 415-931-4927

Floating floor systems

Galleher, Inc.
Corporate Office
9303 Greenleaf Avenue

Santa Fe Springs, CA 90670
Tel: 562-944-8885
Fax: 562-941-3929
E-mail: info@.galleher.com
www.galleher.com

Wood flooring applications

Thurner Hardwood Interiors
221 B Roberts Avenue
Santa Rosa, CA 95401
Tel: 707-575-1063
Fax: 707-575-0456
E-mail: thurnerhardwood@yahoo.com

Flooring

Big Oak Hardwood Floor Company, Inc.
934 Washington Street
San Carlos, CA 94070
Tel: 650-591-8651
Fax: 650-591-8699
E-mail: bigoakfloors@yahoo.com

Drivit plastering materials

Calply Corporate Headquarters
8535 E. Florence Avenue, Suite 100
Downey, CA 90240
Tel: 562-622-7976
Fax: 562-622-7966
E-mail: info@calply.com
www.calply.com

Plastering and building materials, concrete

Shamrock Materials, Inc.
548 Du Bois Street
San Rafael, CA 94901
800-675-1511 or 415-455-1571
Fax: 415-453-3117
E-mail: sales@shamrockmaterials.com
www.shamrockmat.com

Japanese plastering applications
Patrick J. Ruane Inc.
283 Wattis Way
South San Francisco, CA 94080
Tel: 650- 616-7676
Fax: 650-616-4750
E-mail: jim@pjruane.com
www.pjruane.com

Frey Plastering Inc.
898 Vallejo Avenue
Novato, CA 94945
Tel: 415-897-4510
Fax: 415-898-5693
E-mail: barry@freyplastering.com

Architectural woodwork, cabinetry, furniture
Design Woodworking, Inc.
709 N. Sacramento Street
Lodi, CA 95240
Tel: 209-334-6674
Fax: 209-334-1312
E-mail:deswood@pacbell.net
www.deswood.com

Tatami mats, custom-made, custom-cut
Miwa, Inc.
5733 San Leandro St.
Oakland, CA 94621
Tel: 510-261-5999
Fax: 510-261-8666
E-mail: miwa_futon@hotmail.com
www.miwafuton.com

Custom furniture
Jefferson Furniture
Designed by Jefferson Shallenberger
E-mail: js@jeffersonfurniture.com
www.jeffersonfurniture.com

Cabinetry, custom furniture
14th Street Millworks
201 14th Street
Sacramento, CA 95814
Tel: 916-442-6362
Fax: 916-442-6369
E-mail: pg14thst@earthlink.net

Custom-made finish hardware, traditional Japanese hardware
Chisler Manufacturing Company
P.O. Box 15012
Portland, OR 97293
Tel: 503-235-0123
E-mail: daniel@chisler.net
www.chisler.net

Tile and dimensional cut stone
Czarnowski Marble and Granite Works
14964 Applewood Lane
Nevada City, CA 95959
Tel. & Fax: 530-265-2539

Garden Stones
W. Johnson Ornamental Stone
4132 Santa Rosa Avenue
Santa Rosa, CA 95407
Tel. 707-584-7480
Fax: 707-584-4531

Index